Neil J. Anderson

ACTIVE

Skills for **Reading**: Book 1

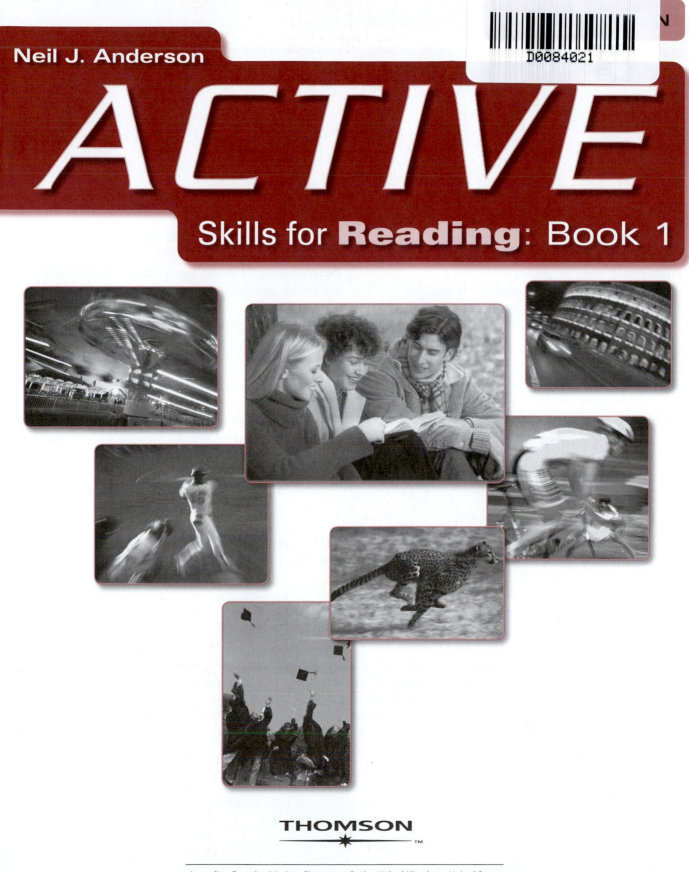

D0084021

THOMSON
™

Australia · Canada · Mexico · Singapore · Spain · United Kingdom · United States

THOMSON

Active Skills for Reading, 2nd Edition, Student Book 1
Neil J. Anderson

Publisher: Christopher Wenger
Director of Content Development: Anita Raducanu
Director of Product Marketing: Amy Mabley
Editorial Manager: Sean Bermingham
Development Editor: Derek Mackrell
Production Editor: Tan Jin Hock
International Marketing Manager: Ian Martin
Sr. Print Buyer: Mary Beth Hennebury

Contributing Writer: Paul MacIntyre
Compositor: CHROME Media Pte. Ltd.
Illustrator: Edwin Ng
Cover/Text Designer: CHROME Media Pte. Ltd.
Printer: Transcontinental
Cover Images: All photos from Photos.com, except amusement park (Index Open) and cyclist (iStockphoto)

Copyright © 2007 by Thomson ELT, a part of The Thomson Corporation. Thomson and the Star logo are trademarks used herein under license.

All rights reserved. No part of this work covered by the copyright hereon may be reproduced or used in any form or by any means—graphic, electronic, or mechanical, including photocopying, recording, taping, Web distribution or information storage and retrieval systems—without the written permission of the publisher.

Printed in Canada.
1 2 3 4 5 6 7 8 9 10   10 09 08 07 06

For more information contact Thomson ELT, 25 Thomson Place, Boston, Massachusetts 02210 USA. You can visit our web site at elt.thomson.com

For permission to use material from this text or product, submit a request online at http://www.thomsonrights.com Any additional questions about permissions can be submitted by e-mail to thomsonrights@thomson.com

ISBN-13: 978-1-4240-0186-6
ISBN-10: 1-4240-0186-2

Photo Credits

Photos.com: pages 8, 9, 11, 12 (top far left, bottom far left), 21 (top right), 26, 27 (center), 37, 47 (top, center), 49 (top right), 55, 61, 65, 69 (all except top left), 80, 106, 112 (right), 115, 121, 125 (all except bottom right), 131; Photo Objects: pages 12 (top center left, bottom center left, bottom center right, bottom far right), 21 (top left, bottom left), 59, 140; iStockphoto: pages 12 (top center right), 16 (all except bottom right), 21 (top center, bottom center, bottom right), 27 (bottom), 47 (bottom), 49 (top left, center), 83, 85, 92 (bottom), 102, 112 (left), 123, 125 (bottom right), 135, 137, 147, 156; Index Open: pages 12 (top far right), 27 (top), 33, 41, 42, 51, 113, 127; Landov: pages 13, 69 (top left), 71, 75, 87, 89, 92 (far left, far right), 103, 107, 109; Mirabell Enterprise: page 16 (bottom right); Faridodin "Fredi" Lajvardi: page 23; www.totallyabsurd.com: page 45; HIRB: page 49 (bottom left, bottom right); Dyson: page 118

Dedication & Acknowledgments

This book is dedicated to Alice McKay Anderson. You will develop into a competent, fluent reader of good books as you read with your parents and family.

ACTIVE Skills for Reading has been a wonderful project to be involved with. I have enjoyed talking with teachers who use the series. I enjoy talking with students who have read passages from the book. When we published the first edition, I had no idea that we would be preparing the second edition so quickly. The success of the book is due to the teachers and students who have been engaged in ACTIVE reading. To the readers of ACTIVE Skills for Reading, I thank you.

I also express great appreciation to Paul MacIntyre for your significant contributions to this edition. It is a great pleasure to work with a committed professional like you. I also express appreciation to Derek Mackrell, Sean Bermingham, and Chris Wenger from Thomson. The support you provided me was unbelievable. I enjoy working with you. Special thanks to Maria O'Conor who played an essential role in the conception of the first edition of ACTIVE Skills for Reading.

Neil J. Anderson

Reviewers for this edition

Chiou-lan Chern National Taiwan Normal University; **Cheongsook Chin** English Campus Institute, Inje University; **Yang Hyun** Jung-Ang Girls' High School; **Li Junhe** Beijing No.4 High School; **Tim Knight** Gakushuin Women's College; **Ahmed M. Motala** University of Sharjah; **Gleides Ander Nonato** Colégio Arnaldo and Centro Universitário Newton Paiva; **Ethel Ogane** Tamagawa University; **Seung Ku Park** Sunmoon University; **Shu-chien, Sophia, Pan** College of Liberal Education, Shu-Te University; **Marlene Tavares de Allmeida** Wordshop Escola de Linguas; **Naowarat Tongkam** Silpakorn University; **Nobuo Tsuda** Konan University; **Hasan Hüseyin Zeyrek** Istanbul Kültür University Faculty of Economics and Administrative Sciences

Reviewers of the first edition

Penny Allan Languages Institute, Mount Royal College; **Jeremy Bishop** Ehwa Women's University; **William E. Brazda** Long Beach City College; **Michelle Buuck** Centennial College; **Chih-min Chou** National Chengchi University; **Karen Cronin** Shinjuku, Tokyo; **Marta O. Dmytrenko-Ahrabian** Wayne State University, English Language Institute; **James Goddard** Kwansei University; **Ann-Marie Hadzima** National Taiwan University; **Diane Hawley Nagatomo** Ochanomizu University; **Carolyn Ho** North Harris College; **Feng-Sheng Hung** National Kaohsiung First University of Science and Technology; **Yuko Iwata** Tokai University; **Johanna E. Katchen** National Tsing Hua University, Department of Foreign Languages; **Peter Kipp** Ehwa Women's University; **Julie Manning** Ritsumeikan Uji High School; **Gloria McPherson** English Language Institute, Seneca College; **Mary E. Meloy Lara** John F. Kennedy Primary School; **Young-in Moon** English Language and Literature Department, The University of Seoul; **Junil Oh** Pukyong National University; **Serdar Ozturk** Terraki Vakfı Okullarj; **Diana Pelyk** Ritsumeikan Asia Pacific University; **Stephen Russell** Meiji Gakuin University; **Consuelo Sañudo** Subsecretaria de Servicios Educativos para el Distrito Federal; **Robin Strickler** Kansai Gaidai University; **Liu Su-Fen** Mingchi Institute of Technology; **Cynthia Cheng-Fang** Tsui National Chengchi University; **Beatrice Vanni** University of Bahcesehir; **Kerry Vrabel** LaGuardia Community College; **Aysen Yurdakul** Buyuk Kolej

Contents

5

Vocabulary Learning Tips

Learning new vocabulary is an important part of learning to be a good reader. Remember that the letter **C** in **ACTIVE Skills for Reading** reminds us to cultivate vocabulary.

1 Decide if the word is worth learning now

As you read you will find many words you do not know. You will slow your reading fluency if you stop at every new word. For example, you should stop to find out the meaning of a new word if:

a. you read the same word many times.

b. the word appears in the heading of a passage, or in the topic sentence of a paragraph—the sentence that gives the main idea of the paragraph.

Review Unit 3 (page 117) gives more practice with this strategy.

2 Record information about new words you decide to learn

Keep a vocabulary notebook in which you write words you want to remember. Complete the following information for words that you think are important to learn:

New word	collect
Translation	收集
Part of speech	verb
Sentence where found	Jamie Oliver collected more than 270,000 signatures from people.
My own sentence	My brother collects stamps.

3 Learn words from the same family

For many important words in English that you will want to learn, the word is part of a word family. As you learn new words, learn words in the family from other parts of speech (nouns, verbs, adjectives, adverbs, etc.).

Noun	happiness
Verb	
Adjective	happy
Adverb	happily

4 Learn words that go with the key word you are learning

When we learn new words, it is important to learn what other words are frequently used with them. These are called collocations. Here is an example from a student's notebook.

take		long		next week
go on	a	two-week		in Italy
need		short	vacation	with my family
have		summer		by myself
		school		

5 Create a word web

A word web is a picture that helps you connect words together and helps you increase your vocabulary. Here is a word web for the word "frightened":

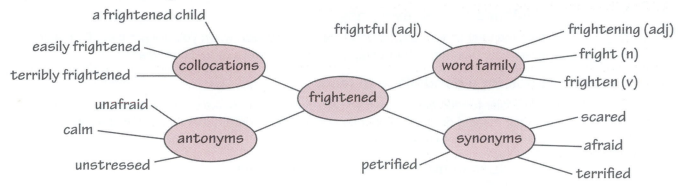

6 Memorize common prefixes, roots, and suffixes

Many English words can be divided into different parts. We call these parts *prefixes*, *roots*, and *suffixes*. A *prefix* comes at the beginning of a word, a *suffix* comes at the end of a word, and the *root* is the main part of the word. In your vocabulary notebook, make a list of prefixes and suffixes as you come across them. On pages 174–175 there is a list of prefixes and suffixes in this book. For example, look at the word "unhappily."

7 Regularly review your vocabulary notebook

You should review the words in your vocabulary notebook very often. The more often you review your list of new words, the sooner you will be able to recognize the words when you see them during reading. Set up a schedule to go over the words you are learning.

8 Make vocabulary flash cards

Flash cards are easy to make, and you can carry them everywhere with you. You can use them to study while you are waiting for the bus, walking to school or work, or eating a meal. You can use the flash cards with your friends to quiz each other. Here is an example of a flash card:

Tips for Fluent Reading

Find time to read every day.

Find the best time of day for you to read. Try to read when you are not tired. By reading every day, even for a short period, you will become a more fluent reader.

Look for a good place to read.

It is easier to read and study if you are comfortable. Make sure that there is good lighting in your reading area and that you are sitting in a comfortable chair. To make it easier to concentrate, try to read in a place where you won't be interrupted.

Use clues in the text to make predictions.

Fluent readers make predictions before and as they read. Use the title, subtitle, pictures, and captions to ask yourself questions about what you are going to read. Find answers to the questions when you read. After reading, think about what you have learned and decide what you need to read next to continue learning.

Establish goals before you read.

Before you read a text, think about the purpose of your reading. For example, do you just want to get a general idea of the passage? Or do you need to find specific information? Thinking about what you want to get from the reading will help you decide what reading skills you need to use.

Notice how your eyes and head are moving.

Good readers use their eyes, and not their heads, when they read. Moving your head back and forth when reading will make you tired. Practice avoiding head movements by placing your elbows on the table and resting your head in your hands. Do you feel movement as you read? If you do, hold your head still as you read. Also, try not to move your eyes back over a text. You should reread part of a text only when you have a specific purpose for rereading, for example, to make a connection between what you read previously and what you are reading now.

Try not to translate.

Translation slows down your reading. Instead of translating new words into your first language, first try to guess the meaning. Use the context (the other words around the new word) and word parts (prefixes, suffixes, and word roots) to help you guess the meaning.

Read in phrases rather than word by word.

Don't point at each word while you read. Practice reading in phrases—groups of words that go together.

Engage your imagination.

Good readers visualize what they are reading. They create a movie in their head of the story they are reading. As you read, try sharing with a partner the kinds of pictures that you create in your mind.

Avoid subvocalization.

Subvocalization means quietly saying the words as you read. You might be whispering the words or just silently saying them in your mind. Your eyes and brain can read much faster than you can speak. If you subvocalize, you can only read as fast as you can say the words. As you read, place your finger on your lips or your throat. Do you feel movement? If so, you are subvocalizing. Practice reading without moving your lips.

Don't worry about understanding every word.

Sometimes, as readers, we think we must understand the meaning of everything that we read. It isn't always necessary to understand every word in a passage in order to understand the meaning of the passage as a whole. Instead of interrupting your reading to find the meaning of a new word, circle the word and come back to it after you have finished reading.

Enjoy your reading.

Your enjoyment of reading will develop over time. Perhaps today you do not like to read in English, but as you read more, you should see a change in your attitude. The more you read in English, the easier it will become. You will find yourself looking forward to reading.

Read as much as you can.

The best tip to follow to become a more fluent reader is to read whenever and wherever you can. Good readers read a lot. They read many different kinds of material: newspapers, magazines, textbooks, websites, and graded readers. To practice this, keep a reading journal. Every day, make a list of the kinds of things you read during the day and how long you read each for. If you want to become a more fluent reader, read more!

Are You an ACTIVE Reader?

Before you use this book to develop your reading skills, think about your reading habits, and your strengths and weaknesses when reading in English. Check the statements that are true for you.

		Start of course	End of course
1	I read something in English every day.	☐	☐
2	I try to read where I'm comfortable and won't be interrupted.	☐	☐
3	I make predictions about what I'm going to read before I start reading.	☐	☐
4	I think about my purpose of reading before I start reading.	☐	☐
5	I keep my head still, and move only my eyes, when I read.	☐	☐
6	I try not to translate words from English to my first language.	☐	☐
7	I read in phrases rather than word by word.	☐	☐
8	I try to picture in my mind what I'm reading.	☐	☐
9	I read silently, without moving my lips.	☐	☐
10	I try to understand the meaning of the passage, and try not to worry about understanding the meaning of every word.	☐	☐
11	I usually enjoy reading in English.	☐	☐
12	I try to read as much as I can, especially outside class.	☐	☐

Follow the tips on pages 8–9. These will help you become a more active reader. At the end of the course, answer this quiz again to see if you have become a more fluent, active reader.

Our Changing Diet

Unit 1

Getting Ready

Discuss the following questions with a partner.

1 What foods do you see in the picture?
2 Which ones do you like? Which ones don't you like?
3 Which ones are good for you?
4 Who is this food for? Where will it be eaten?

Chapter 1: Jamie Oliver's School Dinners

A Match the name of each food with a picture.

a. chicken nuggets	**c.** muffins	**e.** french fries	**g.** soda
b. canned spaghetti	**d.** vegetables	**f.** meat	**h.** fruit

B Which of the foods are good for you? Which aren't good for you? Rank them from 1 (very good for you) to 8 (least good for you). Discuss your answers with a partner.

1 _____ 3 _____ 5 _____ 7 _____

2 _____ 4 _____ 6 _____ 8 _____

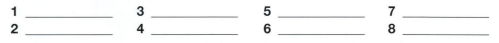

Reading Skill:

Predicting

Before reading, good readers think about what they are going to read. While reading, good readers think about what comes next. This helps them better understand what comes next.

A Look at the title of the article on the next page and the photograph. Try to guess Jamie Oliver's job. Read the first paragraph and see if you were right. Then read the second paragraph.

B Before you read the third paragraph, try to guess some of the junk foods in school dinners. Read the third paragraph and see if you were right. Then read the fourth paragraph.

C Before you read the last paragraph, try to guess where Jamie sent the signatures. Then read the last paragraph and see if you were right.

D Read the passage again and answer the questions that follow.

Lifestyle 3-B

Jamie Oliver's School Dinners

Jamie Oliver is a lively young British chef. He loves to teach us his secrets of cooking and eating. In his first television show, *The Naked Chef*, Oliver taught everyone to make **simple** but delicious food. *In Jamie's Kitchen*, 5 he taught young people how to cook. His next show, *Jamie's School Dinners*, is about changing the foods that students eat.

Oliver saw that some schools in Britain were **serving** junk food—food that is easy to eat but unhealthy. Although it can be delicious, junk food is not very good for 10 you, and it is sometimes **harmful** for your health. Junk food can also harm children, because it doesn't give them the power they need at school. They sometimes can't think well or feel down, and they sometimes **gain weight**.

Some of the junk food that Oliver wants to change is canned spaghetti, chicken nuggets, French fries, soda, and muffins. He **encourages** schools to serve fresh and 15 **healthy** meats, vegetables, and fruits. He helps the school cooks to make healthy dinners without junk food.

People liked Oliver's idea of bringing quality food to schools. Thousands enjoyed his television show. But, Oliver wanted them to do more than just watch. At his *Feed Me Better* website,[1] he **collected** over 270,000 signatures[2] from people. They 20 wanted to stop junk food and put healthy food in schools again.

Oliver sent the signatures to Prime Minister[3] Tony Blair. Prime Minister Blair promised to help change the school **kitchens**, teach school chefs to cook healthy foods, and spend more on school dinners. Thanks to Jamie Oliver, students everywhere in Britain can enjoy more healthy dinners. 25

[1]**Feed Me Better website** www.feedmebetter.com
[2]**signature** a name at the end of a document, usually handwritten, e.g. *Roger Morton*

[3]**prime minister** the leader of the government in some countries, e.g., Japan, Australia, the U.K.

Reading Comprehension:
Check Your Understanding

A The statements below are about the reading. Choose the correct answer to complete each one.

1 Jamie Oliver is a _____.
   a. prime minister   **b.** student   **c.** chef
2 Oliver thinks that _____ is junk food.
   a. meat   **b.** canned spaghetti   **c.** fruit
3 Oliver would probably say that _____ are junk food.
   a. sugar cookies   **b.** vegetables   **c.** eggs
4 In line 12, "*They sometimes can't think well or feel down*," who does "*They*" refer to?
   a. students   **b.** school chefs   **c.** people who watch television

B Number these events 1 to 4 in the order they happened.

_____ Oliver collected over 270,000 signatures.
_____ Oliver sent the signatures to the prime minister.
_____ Oliver made a television show called *Jamie's School Dinners*.
_____ The prime minister promised to help change the school kitchens.

Critical Thinking

C Discuss these questions with your partner.
1 Why do some schools serve junk food to their students?
2 Why did Prime Minister Blair decide to help Jamie Oliver?

Vocabulary Comprehension:
Words in Context

A The words in *italics* are vocabulary items from the reading. Read each question or statement and choose the best answer. Check your answers with a partner.

1 *Simple* foods are usually _____.
   a. easy to make   **b.** difficult to make
2 Does your school *serve* _____?
   a. good chefs   **b.** delicious food
3 If a food is *harmful*, you _____ eat it.
   a. shouldn't   **b.** should
4 You might *gain weight* if you _____.
   a. eat too much   **b.** stop eating
5 Our English teacher *encourages* us _____.
   a. to watch movies in English   **b.** not to do our homework
6 Some examples of *healthy* foods are _____.
   a. french fries and potato chips   **b.** vegetables and fruits
7 The teacher wants to *collect* our homework, so _____.
   a. give it to him now   **b.** take it home after class
8 Javier is _____ in the *kitchen* right now.
   a. running   **b.** cooking

B Complete the sentences using the correct form of the words in *italics* from A.

1 The teacher _____ us to give that man a dollar, because he's collecting for the poor.

2 No, I don't want any potato chips. Is there any healthy food in the _____?

3 You shouldn't eat so much. Gaining too much weight can be very _____.

4 I can only cook things that are very easy to make. I usually _____ very simple food to my family.

A The words in the chart below are all in the reading passage. Match these words with their antonyms from the box. Also, write each word's part of speech in the box (*noun/verb/adjective/preposition*).

healthy   lose   difficult   ~~dislike~~   with   take

	Antonym	Part of Speech
like	*dislike*	*verb*
easy		
gain		
give		
unhealthy		
without		

B Complete the sentences below with the antonyms from the chart in A. Be sure to use the correct form of the word.

1 Cui is a very _____ eater. She only eats fresh fruits and vegetables.
2 Tonight's homework is very, very _____. I can't do it!
3 Little Bobby _____ three muffins from the kitchen before I could stop him.
4 Do you drink coffee _____ sugar or cream?
5 I _____ waiting for the train on cold days.
6 You look beautiful, Samantha! How did you _____ so much weight?

Vocabulary Skill:
Antonyms

An antonym is a word that has the opposite meaning of another word. Sometimes, antonyms are very different words; for example "light" and "dark," "true" and "false." Other times, antonyms are made by adding or changing prefixes or suffixes; for example "happy" and "unhappy," "careless" and "careful." One good way to increase your vocabulary is to learn antonyms.

Chapter 2: Let's Make a Fruit Pavlova!

Discuss the following questions with a partner.

1 Have you ever tried these famous sweets? Do you know who or what they are named after?

Napoleon

Pavlova

Reading Skill:
Scanning

Scanning is looking through a reading for information you need. For example, most people do not read a newspaper from beginning to end. They scan the headlines to find what they want to read. Then they read only certain sections of the newspaper. Scanning can save time, because you only read the information you want. It can also be very helpful when taking a test with questions about information in readings or charts.

Baked Alaska

Mozartkugeln

2 What other famous sweets do you know? Where are they served?

3 What are your favorite sweets? Do you make them in your kitchen at home?

A Scan the reading passage on the next page to find the following information.

   1 Find the list of things you need to make a pavlova. How many different things are needed? _____

   2 How many steps are there in making a pavlova? _____

B In which step is each of these things used? Scan the reading and write the number of the step.

   1 heavy cream   Step _____   **3** mixed fruits   Step _____

   2 vanilla   Step _____   **4** baking sheet   Step _____

C Read the passage again and answer the questions that follow.

Let's Make a Fruit Pavlova!

The pavlova is a delicious dessert from New Zealand and Australia. It was first made in the 1930s for the visit of the great Russian dancer, Anna Pavlova.

Here's what you need:

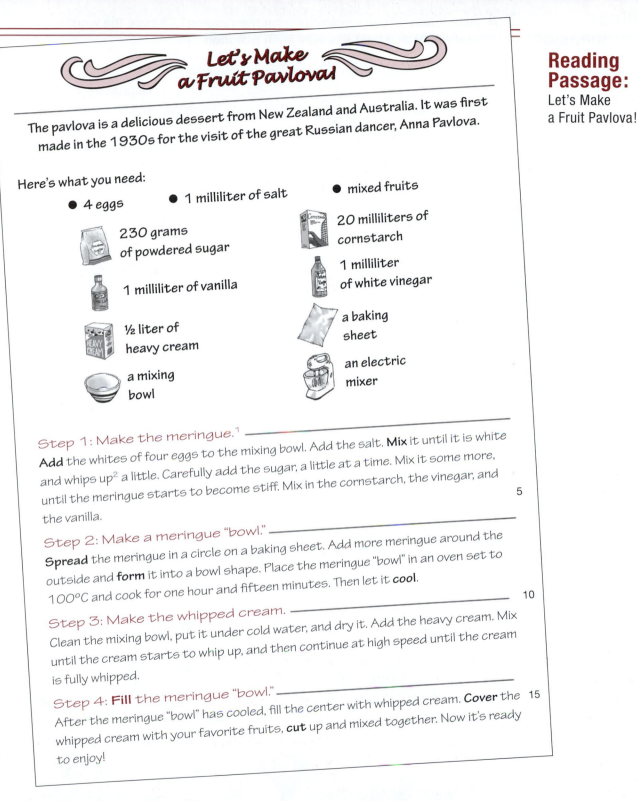

- 4 eggs
- 1 milliliter of salt
- mixed fruits
- 230 grams of powdered sugar
- 20 milliliters of cornstarch
- 1 milliliter of vanilla
- 1 milliliter of white vinegar
- ½ liter of heavy cream
- a baking sheet
- a mixing bowl
- an electric mixer

Step 1: Make the meringue.[1]
Add the whites of four eggs to the mixing bowl. Add the salt. **Mix** it until it is white and whips up[2] a little. Carefully add the sugar, a little at a time. Mix it some more, until the meringue starts to become stiff. Mix in the cornstarch, the vinegar, and the vanilla. 5

Step 2: Make a meringue "bowl."
Spread the meringue in a circle on a baking sheet. Add more meringue around the outside and **form** it into a bowl shape. Place the meringue "bowl" in an oven set to 100°C and cook for one hour and fifteen minutes. Then let it **cool**. 10

Step 3: Make the whipped cream.
Clean the mixing bowl, put it under cold water, and dry it. Add the heavy cream. Mix until the cream starts to whip up, and then continue at high speed until the cream is fully whipped.

Step 4: **Fill** the meringue "bowl."
After the meringue "bowl" has cooled, fill the center with whipped cream. **Cover** the 15 whipped cream with your favorite fruits, **cut** up and mixed together. Now it's ready to enjoy!

[1]**meringue** Meringue is a food made by mixing egg whites for a long time. By adding sugar, you can make it quite hard. It is used in many different desserts.

[2]**whips up** If you mix eggs or cream for a long time, they take on a lot of air; the mixture changes, gets bigger, and feels thicker (less watery). We say it "whips up."

Reading Comprehension:
Check Your Understanding

A **How much do you remember from the reading? Choose the word or statement that best answers each question.**

1 Which of these is not used in making a pavlova?
   a. vinegar   **b.** vanilla   **c.** vegetables

2 An egg has a white part and yellow part. Which part(s) of the egg do you use in making a pavlova?
   a. the white   **b.** the yellow   **c.** the white and the yellow

3 What is at the top of the pavlova?
   a. the meringue "bowl"   **b.** whipped cream   **c.** fruits

4 What is in the middle of the pavlova?
   a. the meringue "bowl"   **b.** whipped cream   **c.** fruits

B **Match each action with its step in the recipe.**

a. Add the heavy cream to the mixing bowl.   _____ Step 1

b. Fill the center of the "bowl" with whipped cream.   _____ Step 2

c. Mix the meringue until it is very stiff.   _____ Step 3

d. Form the meringue into a simple "bowl."   _____ Step 4

Critical Thinking

C **Discuss these questions with your partner.**

1 What parts of the pavlova are healthy? What parts are unhealthy?

2 How could you change this recipe a little to make it healthier?

Vocabulary Comprehension:
Words in Context

A **Match the verbs in the box with the pictures.**

a. add	**c.** spread	**e.** cool	**g.** cover
b. mix	**d.** form	**f.** fill	**h.** cut

B Choose the correct verb to complete these sentences.

1 Please _____ the prime minister's glass with water.
   a. spread   **b.** fill
2 I used the whipped cream to _____ the letters of my name.
   a. cut up   **b.** form
3 I know it's not healthy, but I'm going to _____ more sugar to my coffee.
   a. add   **b.** mix
4 This time, don't _____ your french fries with salt. It's not healthy.
   a. cool   **b.** cover

A Look at the list of irregular verbs below. Write the simple past tense in the chart. Use your dictionary to help you. Can you write any other common irregular past tense verbs?

Base Form	Simple Past	Base Form	Simple Past
break		have	
bring		keep	
buy		know	
come		lose	
cut		put	
do		ride	
eat		spread	
feel		throw	
get		_____	
go		_____	

Regular verbs are formed in the past tense by adding "-ed" to the end of the verb; for example, "play/played," "watch/watched." Irregular verbs are not formed in this way; for example, "shut/shut," "break/broke." Many irregular verbs are very common, so it is important to know them.

B Compare your list with a partner's. Do you notice any patterns in how any of these verbs are formed?

C Now complete each sentence using one of the past tense verbs from A.

1 Ken _____ a pavlova to my party. It was delicious!
2 I collected over 100 old newspapers off the street and I _____ them away.
3 I _____ junk food last night. Eating it just one time can't harm me.
4 To encourage me to call her more, my mother _____ me a new cell phone.
5 Can I use your cell phone for a minute? I _____ mine yesterday.
6 Maria _____ into the kitchen to get something to drink.

Real Life Skill:
Reading Food Labels

In many countries, food labels give important information about what is in the foods we buy. Reading and understanding the labels can help you to eat in a healthier way.

A Read the sentences and write the underlined words next to their definitions below.

The <u>ingredients</u> of onion soup are onions, butter, water, salt, and pepper.
<u>Minerals</u> like iron and calcium are important for your body.
<u>Additives</u> are used to change the color or taste of a food.
<u>Vitamins</u> A and E are good for your body.
This bread contains <u>preservatives</u> so it stays fresh for a longer time.

1 metals that your body needs _____
2 B, C, and D are examples of these _____
3 these keep a food fresh _____
4 things added to a food _____
5 the things used to make a food _____

B Read the labels for these food bars and complete the sentences below.

No added sugar—no additives

High protein for an active life
N-R-G BAR

100% of the 10 vitamins and minerals you need every day

The taste you love...
YUMMY BAR

Ingredients: sugar, honey, butter, cocoa, peanuts, salt, preservatives

A complete meal— only 200 calories
SLIM QUICK BAR
Strawberry-yogurt flavor

Fiber and protein to help you feel full longer— vitamins to help you lose weight faster!

1 A seven-year-old child would eat _____
   because _____
2 A person trying to lose weight would eat _____
   because _____
3 A football player would eat _____
   because _____

What Do You Think?

1 Many people think cooking at home is a healthy way to eat. How can a person be a healthy eater without cooking at home?
2 Should children and older people all eat the same foods? How should the foods we eat change as we age?
3 Vegetarians—people who don't eat meat—are becoming more common in some countries. Why do you think so?

Inventions

Getting Ready

Discuss the following questions with a partner.

A Match the inventions with their names.

> **a.** dishwasher   **c.** computer mouse   **e.** vacuum cleaner
> **b.** submarine   **d.** microwave oven   **f.** disposable camera

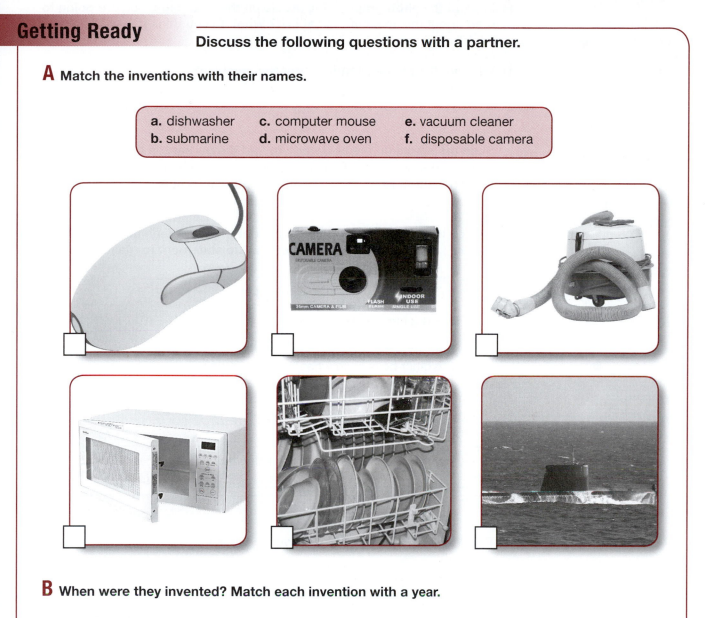

B When were they invented? Match each invention with a year.

1 dishwasher   _____   **a.** 1986
2 vacuum cleaner   _____   **b.** 1906
3 computer mouse   _____   **c.** 1968
4 microwave oven   _____   **d.** 1886
5 submarine   _____   **e.** 1624
6 disposable camera _____   **f.** 1946

C What inventions do you use every day?

Before You Read:
"Stinky" the Machine

A Look at the photograph in the article on the next page. You are going to read about this machine. What is it? What do you think it is used for?

B Who are the people standing near the machine?

Reading Skill:
Reading for Details

When we read for details, we read every word carefully and think carefully about the meaning. It is usually best to read for details when we are looking for information in a part of the reading; for example, when answering questions for a test.

A Scan the article on the next page to find the paragraph that tells what happened when students traveled with their machines to California. Read this paragraph. Then answer the questions in B.

B Decide if the following statements about the paragraph are true (*T*) or false (*F*). If you check (✓) false, correct the statement to make it true.

	T	F
1 MIT is a famous high school. _____		
2 The other boys cried when they saw "Stinky." _____		
3 "Stinky" had a very strong smell. _____		
4 "Stinky" was the best machine in the competion. _____		

C Read the article again, then answer the questions that follow.

Technology 5-D

The High School That **Beat** MIT

At Carl Hayden High School in Phoenix, Arizona in the United States, four poor Mexican boys, Christian Arcega, Lorenzo Santillan, Luis Aranda, and Oscar Vazquez, worked together on a strange electric machine, encouraged by their teacher Allan Cameron. They collected only $800 from people in the town to build it. They used pipes, cameras, computer parts, and whatever they could find. All the other students were **curious** about it. They wanted to know what it was. The machine was like a very small submarine. It could move around in a swimming pool.[1] The boys could control its movements from outside the pool.

Carl Hayden had been **invited** to a **competition** of high schools and universities. The schools were from the United States and Canada. The school that could build the best machine would be the winner. Many students came from schools that gave them lots of money and support. The Carl Hayden boys had hardly any **support** and very little money.

Students from eleven schools traveled with their machines to the University of California, including students from the famous university, MIT. When students saw the machine made by the Carl Hayden boys, some of them laughed. Its name was "Stinky" because it had a very strong **smell**. But, when the competition started, they saw that "Stinky" was no **joke**. It did better than all the other **machines**, including MIT's, and it took first place in the competition.

Since winning, the boys from Carl Hayden have become famous. People have even offered them money for college, and a movie producer has asked them if it is OK to make a movie to tell their story.

[1]**swimming pool** a large hole in the ground that is made and filled with water so people can swim in it.

Reading Comprehension:
Check Your Understanding

A These statements are about the article. Choose the correct answer to complete each one.

1 _____ encouraged the four boys from Carl Hayden High School.
   a. MIT   **b.** Their teacher   **c.** Other students
2 The Carl Hayden team had _____ the other competing teams.
   a. more money than   **b.** less money than   **c.** the same amount of money as
3 The Carl Hayden High School team's machine finished _____.
   a. behind MIT   **b.** in first place   **c.** with MIT
4 After winning the competition, the boys _____.
   a. became famous   **b.** made a movie   **c.** sold "Stinky"

B In which paragraph (1–4) of the article can you find the following information? Write the number. You may use any number more than once.

1 what the boys used to make the machine   _____
2 offers of money to the boys   _____
3 what happened at the competition   _____
4 why the boys built "Stinky"   _____

Critical Thinking

C Discuss these questions with your partner.
1 Why do you think the Carl Hayden team was able to beat MIT?
2 What do you think will happen to the four boys?

Vocabulary Comprehension:
Word Definitions

A Look at the list of words from the reading. Match each one with a definition on the right.

1 beat   _____   **a.** wanting to know
2 competition   _____   **b.** ask someone to come
3 curious   _____   **c.** many people together, all trying to win
4 invite   _____   **d.** help
5 joke   _____   **e.** words that make people laugh
6 machine   _____   **f.** what our noses can tell us
7 smell   _____   **g.** win against another person or team
8 support   _____   **h.** a car, a clock, a mixer, etc.

B Use the correct form of the words in A to complete the sentences.

1 Cover your nose! There's a very bad _____ coming from the kitchen.
2 I played games with my friend last night. I _____ her every time!
3 Juanita is always asking personal questions. She's a very _____ person.
4 I've _____ twenty people to a pool party tomorrow, so don't forget to fill the swimming pool.

A Add prefixes to the word parts below by writing them in the correct columns.

-municate	-nect	-pare	-fort	-tain	-mon

com

con

"Com-" and "con-" are prefixes that mean "with" or "together." Remembering what these prefixes mean can help you to understand more words.

B Now match each word from A with a definition below.

1 to join or link together _____
2 normal; ordinary _____
3 to have, include in _____
4 to talk to and understand others _____
5 to look at how two or more things are the same or different _____
6 to help someone feel better when something bad happens _____

C Use each of the words above to complete the following sentences. Be sure to use the correct form of the word.

1 Before you buy new shoes, you should _____ prices at another shoe store.
2 One of the problems with people today is that they do not _____ with each other about their thoughts and feelings.
3 We cut a door through this wall, so now, the kitchen is _____ to the dining room.
4 I had to _____ my son when he failed his test.
5 This soup already _____ salt, but I added a little more. I like salty food.
6 John is a very _____ name for a man.

Chapter 2: *The Most Useful Inventions*

Before You Read:
Useful Inventions

A Look at this list of useful inventions. Work with a partner to add three more to the list.

Invention	Rank
the telephone	_____
the car	_____
the airplane	_____
paper	_____
the Internet	_____
_____	_____
_____	_____
_____	_____

B With your partner, rank the inventions from 1 (most useful) to 8 (least useful).

Reading Skill:
Scanning

When we scan we look for specific information in what we are reading. We move our eyes quickly over the page, and we do not read the information that we are not looking for. In Chapter 2 of Unit 1 we used scanning to find information in a recipe, and we mentioned that scanning is useful when taking tests. It is also very useful for getting information from websites.

A Match the names with the message dates. Scan the website on the next page for the information.

1 Jorge _____   **a.** April 13
2 Cindy _____   **b.** April 14
3 Kazuo _____   **c.** April 15

B Match the names with the inventions. Again, scan the website on the next page for the information.

1 Jorge _____   **a.** electricity
2 Cindy _____   **b.** the Internet
3 Kazuo _____   **c.** air conditioner

C Read the passage again and answer the questions that follow.

http://www.ACTIVEblog.heinle.com

Blog ⇨ TheMostUsefulInventions

The Most Useful Inventions
The Invention Blog: A Place for People to Share Opinions

Today's question is:
What do you think is the most useful invention of all time?

Posted by Cindy Wu on Saturday, April 13
There are many—the train, the car, and the airplane are
useful machines, but these are not my choices. For an   5
everyday, useful invention, I **vote** for the air conditioner.
I live in Taipei, and **during** the summer the **temperature**
can be 35 degrees Celsius or more. It's so hot! I'm not
joking when I say that, without an air conditioner, people
here cannot work or study. A lot of people might also get   10
sick without cool air.

Posted by Jorge on Sunday, April 14
The most useful invention of all time is **surely** the Internet.
We can now reach people and do business faster. I own
a clothing store in Mexico City, and there's a lot of   15
competition. I also have a website. Now, people from all
over the world can buy my clothing using my website.
I can **keep in touch** with friends and family in Mexico and
around the world using e-mail. It's faster than usual mail,
and it's cheaper than using the phone!   20

Posted by Kazuo on Monday, April 15
Jorge, I also think that the Internet is **useful**. But, in my
opinion, there is an "invention" that is even more important,
and that's electricity. Of course, this isn't a man-made
invention, but people like Benjamin Franklin and   25
Alessandro Volta learned how to use it. Without electricity,
many of the world's most important inventions would not work.

Reading Comprehension:
Check Your Understanding

A The statements below are about the reading. Choose the correct answer to complete each one.

1 For Cindy, the air conditioner is the most useful because _____.
   a. her apartment doesn't smell very good
   b. she lives in a very hot place
   c. she often gets sick

2 Jorge says that the Internet helps him to _____.
   a. buy clothing from all around the world
   b. keep in touch with family and friends
   c. use the telephone more cheaply

3 Kazuo thinks electricity is the most useful because _____.
   a. many machines cannot work without it
   b. Benjamin Franklin learned how to use it
   c. it isn't really an invention

B Who is the information true for? Check (✓) Cindy, Jorge, or Kazuo.

	Cindy	Jorge	Kazuo
1 chose an invention that people didn't make			
2 mentioned trains, cars, and planes			
3 works in a competitive business			
4 can't work in hot temperatures			
5 has a website			

Critical Thinking

C Discuss these questions with your partner.
1 Do you agree with Cindy, Jorge, or Kazuo about the most useful invention?
2 If someone invited you to post your opinion on the Internet, would you like to do it? Why or why not?

Vocabulary Comprehension:
Words in Context

A The words in *italics* are vocabulary items from the reading. Complete each statement with the best answer.

1 You might get *sick* if you eat food that is _____.
   a. healthy   b. harmful

2 If you do something *during* class, you do it _____.
   a. at the same time as the class   b. a little before the class

3 If someone says, "It will *surely* rain," they mean there is _____.
   a. some question it will rain   b. no question it will rain

4 An *opinion* is _____.
   a. one person's idea   b. an idea that is true for everyone

5 When we *keep in touch* with someone, we _____.
   a. compliment them   b. communicate with them

6 When we *vote* for a new president, we _____.

    a. choose a new president   **b.** help a new president

7 The *temperature* in this room is _____.

    a. 35 milliliters   **b.** 35 degrees Celsius

8 English is a very *useful* language because _____.

    a. many people speak it   **b.** is very difficult

B Complete the paragraph with the correct form of words in *italics* from A.

It was so hot yesterday! I think the **(1)** _____ was nearly 40 degrees Celsius. In the office where I work we have air conditioning, but it wasn't very **(2)** _____. Three people got **(3)** _____ and had to go home —they weren't very healthy, I'm afraid. The man on the television said that it would **(4)** _____ cool down next week, so we won't need much electricity for our air conditioner then.

Vocabulary Skill:
The Suffixes *-ful* and *-less*

A Look at the root words below. Add the suffixes *-ful* and *-less* to each one to make positive and negative antonyms. Write the words on the correct line. Can you add any more words?

> use-   care-   thought-   help-   rest-

Positive: _____

Negative: _____

B Now look at the definitions below and match a word from A to each one. Be careful; not all of the words will be used.

1 thinking of others _____

2 moving around a lot; not relaxed _____

3 taking time and trouble; thinking about things _____

4 not able to do anything _____

5 calm, peaceful, relaxed _____

6 having no purpose _____

C Now use some of the words from A to complete the sentences below.

1 Be very _____ not to mix the eggs too quickly. If you do, they will whip up, and we don't want that.

2 We felt so _____ when the other team beat us. There was nothing I could do.

3 This knife is _____! It doesn't cut anything.

4 That was very _____ of you to talk about Carol's weight. You know she's trying to lose some!

5 Aki didn't sleep all last night. He was so _____ that he got up at 3 A.M. to study.

6 Ming was very _____ and added salt to his coffee instead of sugar.

The suffixes "-ful" and "-less" have opposite meanings. When "-ful" is added to a word it means "with" or "full of." When "-less" is added it means "without." Some root words can have both suffixes added to make adjectives that are antonyms. For example, "useful" describes something that is helpful and has a use. "Useless" describes something that is not helpful or does not have a use.

Real Life Skill:

Dictionary Skills:
Identifying Parts
of Speech

In English, the
same word can be
used as several
different parts
of speech, with
different meanings;
for example, "work"
can mean "to do a
job" when used as
a verb. When used
as a noun, it means
"a job."

A Look at the dictionary abbreviations for the parts of speech below. Read
the three examples for each one, then add two more examples of your own.

n.	noun	Jamie, bowl, machine, _____, _____
v.	verb	fill, support, invite, _____, _____
adv.	adverb	surely, carefully, happily, _____, _____
adj.	adjective	simple, healthy, curious, _____, _____
prep.	preposition	during, after, in, _____, _____

B Look at the dictionary entries below. Read the paragraph that follows
and write the correct abbreviation on the line to show the part of
speech for each word.

cool	/kuːl/	*v.* to make the temperature of something go down; *adj.* having a low temperature
cover	/kʌvə/	*n.* something that fits on top of a can, jar, etc; *v.* to put something over another thing
form	/fɔːm/	*n.* the shape of something; *v.* to change the shape of something
joke	/dʒəʊk/	*n.* words that make people laugh; *v.* to say something to make people laugh

My girlfriend and I were sitting outside on a nice, cool
(_____) day. We looked up at the clouds in the sky.
Sometimes we saw the forms (_____) of animals. I joked
(_____) that I could see her in the sky too. She laughed.
Then there was a very nice smell. Her mother had put two
apple pies outside to cool (_____). My girlfriend got up
and went over to the pies. She wanted to cover (_____)
them so that nobody would touch them. Later, we shared a
piece of delicious pie.

What Do You Think?

1 What were some of the very first inventions?
2 Who are some famous inventors? Would you like to be an inventor?
3 What are some inventions that might be made in the future?

North America

Europe

Asia

Africa

South America

Australasia

Antarctica

Getting Ready

Discuss the following questions with a partner.

1 What countries have you visited in your life? Write them on the map.
2 What countries would you like to visit? Write them on the map and underline them.
3 What country would you choose for a year of study abroad? Write it on the map and circle it.
4 Why would you choose to study in that country?

Chapter 1: Choosing to Study Abroad

Before You Read:
Planning to Study

A **Name five English-speaking countries.**

1 _____

2 _____

3 _____

4 _____

5 _____

B **Look at these reasons for studying abroad. Add two more of your own. Discuss your answers with a partner.**

1 experience life in a different country

2 make friends

3 go sightseeing

4 be able to speak English all day

5 get a better job

6 get ready to live abroad

7 _____

8 _____

Reading Skill:
Using Subtitles to Predict Content

Sometimes reading passages are divided into paragraphs that have subtitles. We can use our knowledge of the topic and these subtitles to predict some of the ideas that may be in the reading.

A **Look at the advertisement on the next page. Read only the title and the subtitles of the four main paragraphs. What ideas do you think will be in each paragraph? Fill in the chart below with your predictions.**

Subtitle	Ideas
Why do it?	
Making the right choice	
Getting ready to go	
Once you are there	

B **Scan each of the four main paragraphs. Are any of your ideas in the chart the same as the ideas in the advertisement?**

C **Now read through the advertisement and answer the questions that follow.**

Study Abroad with TraveLingua!

Every year, thousands of students choose to study **abroad** for the summer, six months, a year, or longer. Studying abroad can be an **exciting experience** for many people. Let our service help you get started.

Why do it?
Living in another country will help you learn a language and learn about the **culture** of another   5
land. You will see the world in a new way and learn more about yourself. Studying abroad is also **excellent** training for the working world. Many companies today want employees who speak a second language or who have experienced living or working in another country.

Making the right choice
To choose the right country or school, ask yourself these questions: How long do I want to   10
study abroad? Do I want to live with a host family,[1] with roommates, or alone? How much do I want to pay?

Getting ready to go
Get your passport and visa[2] early! Before you go, learn as much of the language as you can, and read about the customs of your host country. Also, talk with people who have experience   15
studying abroad. Call the school to make sure someone can meet you when you get there. And **make sure** to bring some local money and a credit card.

Once you are there
Be curious and open to meeting new people and having new experiences. Don't expect to always be **comfortable**. After the first few weeks it's usual to feel a little homesick.[3] You'll   20
miss your family and friends. Remember that it takes time to get used to a new place with new customs. Talk to your new friends and write about your feelings. Try to keep in touch with the people back home. Always keep an open mind and you'll succeed.

[1]**host family** a family that students live with while they are abroad
[2]**visa** papers or stamp in your passport that let you to enter and stay in another country
[3]**homesick** feeling of missing one's home, family, and friends while traveling or abroad

Reading Comprehension:
Check Your Understanding

A The statements below are about the advertisement. Choose the correct answer to complete each one.

1 When you study in another country you can _____.
   a. learn a language   **b.** train for the working world   **c.** both a and b

2 According to the advertisement, one question to think about when choosing the right school or country is _____.
   a. Do I need better language skills before I go?
   b. What is the local food like?
   c. Do I want to live with roommates?

3 The advertisement suggests that you should take _____ with you.
   a. a credit card   **b.** common customs   **c.** books

4 Many students will feel _____ after a few weeks.
   a. afraid   **b.** happy   **c.** homesick

B Number the items 1–4 in the order they should follow according to the advertisement.

   a. _____ talk to your new friends and write about your feelings
   b. _____ decide how long you want to study abroad
   c. _____ get your passport and visa
   d. _____ phone the school to ask for someone to meet you

Critical Thinking

C Discuss these questions with your partner.
   1 What kinds of people might use TraveLingua?
   2 What advice can you add to the "Getting ready to go" and "Once you are there" sections of the advertisement?

Vocabulary Comprehension:
Odd Word Out

A The words in *italics* are vocabulary items from the advertisement. For each group, circle the word that does not belong.

1	traditions	*culture*	people
2	*experience*	knowledge	competition
3	homesick	*comfortable*	relaxed
4	*exciting*	interesting	useful
5	sick	great	*excellent*
6	opinion	*abroad*	overseas
7	*make sure*	work	check
8	dislike	hate	*miss*

B Complete the sentences below using words in *italics* from A.

1 The _____ here is very different from that in my country.
2 _____ to collect the homework from the students after class.
3 I really _____ my family. I'm going to call them tonight.
4 This chair is so _____ that I'm falling asleep in it!

A Look at how some compound words are made.

Some join two nouns together to form one word:

| room + mate = **roommate** |

Some put two nouns together to talk about a single thing:

| air + conditioner = **air conditioner** |

Others join adjectives and nouns together to make one word, or a hyphenated word:

| home + sick = **homesick**   man + made = **man-made** |

Vocabulary Skill:
Compound Words

Compound words are formed by putting two words together to form a new word, for example, "man-made."

B Match a word from the box below with the nouns and adjectives listed to form compound words. Decide which form each compound word has.

| sick   book   made   credit   room   air |

1 _____ card
2 man-_____
3 _____ conditioner
4 note_____
5 _____mate
6 home_____

C Now complete the sentences below using the correct compound word. Be sure to use the correct form of the word.

1 Excuse me, can I pay for this by _____?
2 It's very cool in here. Please turn off the _____.
3 The first time I went abroad I got _____ after only one month.
4 One toy company sells _____ dogs. They are computerized machines.
5 My _____ all work on Saturday, so I am at home alone today.
6 Can I have some paper to write on? I've left my _____ at home.

Chapter 2: My Travel Journal

Before You Read:
Writing a Journal

A Scan the travel journal on the next page. Look only at the title, the subtitles, and the photographs. Then answer the following questions.

1 Who wrote the travel journal? _____

2 Where did the person travel to? _____

3 How long was the person traveling?
   a. more than one month   **b.** less than one month

B Discuss your answers, and the following questions, with a partner.

1 Would you enjoy reading someone's travel journal? Why?

2 Do you keep a travel journal or would you like to? Why or why not?

Reading Skill:
Reading for Details

When reading for details, we read every word and make sure to understand the meaning. Reading for details is especially useful when we need to get information from one part of a larger reading. We can scan the reading for the part we need to read for details. We often need to do this when taking tests.

A Check (✓) three things Lily wrote about on October 20.

1 ☐ It is difficult for her to talk to her classmates.
2 ☐ Her English is improving too fast.
3 ☐ She isn't making lots of friends.
4 ☐ She can't understand her teacher.
5 ☐ She can't take the bus.
6 ☐ She has trouble understanding people on the bus.

B Check (✓) three things Lily did on October 27.

1 ☐ She wrote for the student newspaper.
2 ☐ She met a French woman.
3 ☐ She talked about her experiences in the United States.
4 ☐ She met a Japanese man.
5 ☐ She walked around the city.
6 ☐ She went to a party.

C Now read through the journal and answer the questions that follow.

Me—Lily

New York!

My Travel Journal

September 13

I arrived in New York two weeks ago. I am writing this **journal** for one of my classes. My teacher says it is a good way for me to **practice** writing in English and to write about my experiences here in the United States. So far, I like New York and my school. I have three classes a day. Most of my classmates come from Japan, Korea, Spain, Germany, and Brazil. There aren't many Taiwanese students, so I have to use English most of the time. I am learning a lot! I am living in student housing, and I have my own comfortable room.

October 20

My English is hopeless! I was on the bus this morning and a man spoke to me, but I **hardly** understood him. I was so **embarrassed**. Why is my English **improving** so slowly? I want to make **lots** of American friends, but this isn't happening so easily. I feel **shy**, and it is hard for me to talk to some people, even my classmates! I like them, but sometimes I can't understand them very well. I think I'm feeling homesick. I miss my friends and family.

October 27

I went to a school party last Friday and it was **awesome**. I talked with a Japanese man named Kenji, and an Italian woman named Carla. We talked about our countries' customs and our experiences in the States so far. We are going to walk around the city together this weekend. Also, Kenji wants me to write for the student newspaper here at school. Maybe things are getting better!

Reading Comprehension:
Check Your Understanding

A **How much do you remember from the reading? Choose the best answer for each question or statement below.**

1 Whose idea was it for Lily to keep a journal?
- **a.** her classmates'
- **b.** her teacher's
- **c.** Kenji's

2 The students in Lily's class are _____.
- **a.** mostly from Taiwan
- **b.** all Japanese and Italian
- **c.** from different countries

3 Lily said she was embarrassed because _____.
- **a.** she took the wrong bus
- **b.** she couldn't understand someone
- **c.** she was depressed and homesick

4 At the end of October, Lily was feeling _____.
- **a.** embarrassed
- **b.** depressed and homesick
- **c.** better than before

B **Number these events 1 to 4 in the order they happened.**

_____ A man spoke to her on the bus.

_____ Lily arrived in New York.

_____ Lily's teacher asked her to keep a travel journal.

_____ She went to a party.

Critical Thinking

C **Discuss these questions with your partner.**

1 Lily is studying English with students from many different countries. Do you think this is better than studying with students who are all from her own country? Why or why not?

2 Like Lily, everyone makes mistakes when they are learning a new language. Mistakes are important for learning. What can we do to not feel embarrassed about them?

Vocabulary Comprehension:
Words in Context

A **The words in *italics* are vocabulary items from Lily's journal. Read each question or statement and choose the correct answer.**

1 If Jin-Song's friends think his sneakers are *awesome*, they probably _____.
- **a.** want some, too
- **b.** don't like them at all.

2 Because I have *lots* of money, I _____.
- **a.** can't buy too many things
- **b.** can give some to my friends

3 I think my English is *improving* because _____.
- **a.** I can understand American movies now
- **b.** everyone always smiles when I speak

4 Jun was really *embarrassed* during class yesterday because _____.

   a. she forgot to bring her homework   **b.** she got an "A" on the test

5 An excellent way to *practice* speaking English is _____.

   a. go to American movies   **b.** speak English after class with classmates

6 Sandra uses a *journal* to _____.

   a. write things that happen to her   **b.** read the news

7 Our team *hardly* beat the other team—the score was 101 for us, _____ for them.

   a. 70   **b.** 100

8 Yuki is really *shy* in front of the class. Her _____.

   a. face and ears get red   **b.** way of speaking is excellent

B **Answer these questions. Share your ideas with a partner.**

1 What places do you know that have *lots* of trees? _____

2 How do you *practice* English? _____

3 What actor or actress do you think is *awesome*? _____

4 How have you *improved* in the past few years? _____

A **Look at the list of verbs below. Make adjectives that describe feelings by adding *-ed*. Write them in the chart. Can you think of any other words to add to the chart?**

Verb	Adjective
depress	
embarrass	
excite	
tire	
worry	
interest	

B **Complete the paragraph below using adjectives from the chart above.**

Healthy Living Gym

Do you feel _____(depress)? Are you _____(tire) all the time? Are you _____(worry) about your health? You may not be getting enough exercise. Healthy Living Gym encourages you to come in and start exercising today. You'll feel _____(excite) about losing weight and looking great. Are you _____(interest)? Don't be _____ _____(embarrass)! Come in today!

Vocabulary Skill:

Adjectives Ending in *-ed*

Some adjectives that describe how we are feeling end in "-ed." Most of these adjectives come from verbs with the same root word. For example, from the verb "interest" we can make the adjective "interested" by adding "-ed." For verbs that end in "y," we change the "y" to an "i" and add "-ed."

Real Life Skill:
Writing an English Journal

Writing a journal is a good way to remember your thoughts and experiences, keep a record of what you learn, and practice your English writing skills. You can keep a journal of all your daily experiences, or about one subject such as travel, books you read, or how your studies are going.

A Read the following tips for keeping a journal.

Tips for keeping a journal
- Use a notebook with lined paper that gives you lots of space for writing.
- Make sure to include the date every time you write in your journal.
- Write about things that are interesting or important to you.
- Try to make a regular time for writing in your journal—for example, three times a week after English class, or every evening.
- Don't worry about grammar and spelling.
- Read over your journal entry before you give it to your teacher.

B Now read this journal entry.

Tuesday, October 15
Today, I finished reading an exciting book called "The Perfect Storm."
It was about a group of men on a fishing boat that sank in a very bad storm. The book talked about their families and friends, and it was a really sad story. I would like to see the movie that was made about this story. Tomorrow I will start reading a Harry Potter book.

C Now write a journal entry about an interesting book or story that you have read.

——————————— (date)

What Do You Think?

1 If you got homesick abroad, what five things would you do to make yourself feel better?
2 Make a list of five good things about studying abroad. Share your ideas with a partner. Who do you know that has studied abroad? How did their experience change them?

Fluency Strategy: *SQ3R*

SQ3R is a simple way to help you be a better, more fluent reader and to increase your reading comprehension. SQ3R stands for **S**urvey, **Q**uestion, **R**ead, **R**eview, **R**ecite.

Survey

Survey is similar to the A in the ACTIVE approach to reading; Activate prior knowledge. When you survey, you prepare yourself by skimming quickly through the text you will read. You read the title, the headings, and the first sentence in each section of the passage. You look for and read words that are written in **bold** or *italic*. Look at any pictures and read any captions. Through the survey you prepare yourself to read.

Look below at extracts from the passage on the next page, "The 'Freshman Fifteen,'" then go on to the Question section.

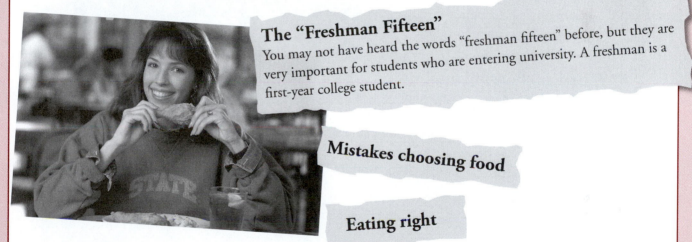

The "Freshman Fifteen"

You may not have heard the words "freshman fifteen" before, but they are very important for students who are entering university. A freshman is a first-year college student.

Mistakes choosing food

Eating right

Question

After the survey, but before you read, ask yourself **questions**. "What do I want to learn as I read?"

Based on your survey of "The 'Freshman Fifteen,'" write two or three questions that you hope to answer as you read.

1 _____

2 _____

3 _____

Read

Following the survey and question stage of SQ3R you **read**. You focus on comprehending the material. You move your eyes fluently through the material.

Read "The 'Freshman Fifteen.'" As you read, keep in mind the 12 tips on pages 8 and 9. By combining those tips and SQ3R you will improve your reading fluency.

The "Freshman Fifteen"

You may not have heard the words "freshman fifteen" before, but they are very important for students who are entering university. A freshman is a

5 first-year college student. "Fifteen" refers to fifteen pounds—the fifteen pounds added to a student's weight in his or her first year. There are a number of reasons why first-year university students gain

10 weight; but it's encouraging to know that freshmen don't have to add these harmful fifteen pounds.

Mistakes choosing food

University kitchens serve many kinds of food. Some students choose unhealthy food, because

15 now their parents are not nearby to help them choose. Some students visit the kitchen many times while studying. Late at night, some students get harmful fast food such as french fries and chicken nuggets with soda to drink. Students also have less time for walking, running, and doing sports because of their schoolwork.

Eating right

20 If you're careful, you don't have to add fifteen pounds. Here are some ideas:

- Think more about what you eat.
- Eat plenty of vegetables and healthy meats.
- Don't eat desserts full of sugar; have fruit after dinner.
- Try not to eat so much junk food while you study.

25 - It's all right to have a little fast food sometimes—but not often.
- Write down the foods you eat.
- Walk, run, do sports—move and you will feel better!

Remember that the "freshman fifteen" can happen to anyone. Talk to your friends about it. Together, try to eat healthy food and not to eat junk food. Walking, running, and playing

30 sports is always more fun with friends. Help each other and you can have a healthy and happy freshman year.

Review

After you read, you review. During the review stage of SQ3R you review the questions that you asked yourself prior to reading.

A Did you find answers to your questions? Write the answers below.

1 _____

2 _____

3 _____

B Check how well you understood the passage by answering the following questions.

1 The "freshman fifteen" is
   a. weight that high school students gain.
   b. fifteen pounds of food that first-year students eat.
   c. weight that first-year university students can gain.
   d. fifteen students who eat junk food.

2 The main idea of this reading is to
   a. get students ready to gain fifteen pounds.
   b. sell healthy food to new students.
   c. help new university students not to gain fifteen pounds.
   d. show the mistakes students make in choosing food.

3 Which of these ideas about eating right is not mentioned in the reading?
   a. eating vegetables
   b. having a little fast food
   c. mixing vegetables and fruits
   d. writing down foods

4 Which of these mistakes students make choosing food is not mentioned in the reading?
   a. choosing unhealthy food
   b. visiting the kitchen while studying
   c. getting fast food at night
   d. eating too much chocolate

5 Why do students choose unhealthy food?
   a. Their parents aren't nearby.
   b. They like to eat junk food and desserts.
   c. They want to eat while they study.
   d. all of the above

6 Which of these ideas would the writer of the reading probably agree with?
   a. You should never eat junk food.
   b. Not eating unhealthy foods is easier with friends' help.
   c. Gaining fifteen pounds can help you study better.
   d. Some students can eat anything they want.

Recite

The final step of SQ3R is to **recite** what you have learned while reading. The important thing is that you close your book and remember what you have read. You can recite in different ways.

- **If you are alone, write down the key information that you learned as you were reading.**
- **If you have a partner, talk to him or her about what you have read.**

Self Check

Write a short answer to each of the following questions.

1. Have you ever used the SQ3R method before?

   Yes   No   I'm not sure.

2. Do you think SQ3R is helpful? Why or why not?

   _____

   _____

3. Will you practice SQ3R in your reading outside of English class?

   _____

   _____

4. Which of the six reading passages in units 1–3 did you enjoy most? Why?

   _____

   _____

5. Which of the six reading passages in units 1–3 was easiest? Which was most difficult? Why?

   _____

   _____

6. What have you read in English outside of class recently?

   _____

   _____

7. What distractions do you face when you read? What can you do to minimize those distractions?

   _____

   _____

8. How will you try to improve your reading fluency from now on?

   _____

   _____

   _____

Review Reading 1: *Four Funny Inventions*

Fluency Practice

Time yourself as you read through the passage. Try to read as fluently as you can. Record your time in the Reading Rate Chart on page 176. Then answer the questions on the following page.

http://www.asrinventions.com/funny

Blog ➾ FourFunnyInventions

Four Funny Inventions

Time Temp Glasses

Are you a person who wants to know the time and temperature during the day? You might like *Time Temp Glasses*. These special glasses show the time above your right eye and the temperature above your left eye. It is surely easier than wearing a wristwatch, and
5 you never have to guess the temperature.

Alarm Fork

Do you eat too quickly? Do you eat too much? How can the *Alarm Fork* help you? Aren't you curious? Well, this special fork has two lights: one green and one red. When the green light is on, it's OK to take a bite of food. The fork "knows" when you take a bite,
10 and soon the red light goes on. Wait for the green light before you take another bite.

Smell This

How do you know if your breath smells nice, or if it smells bad? It's difficult to know, because it's very hard to smell the air that comes out of your own mouth. *Smell This* is useful for this situation. *Smell This* covers your nose and your mouth, so it is easy to
15 smell the air that comes out of your mouth. Does your breath smell nice, or do you need a piece of gum?

Banana Suitcase

Has this ever happened to you? You put a banana in your bag lunch in the morning, and when you open the bag at noon, the
20 banana looks like someone drove a car over it. If you put your banana in the *Banana Suitcase*, this will never happen. It keeps a banana safe, delicious, and looking like a banana!

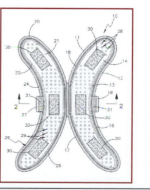

The Banana Suitcase
from www.totallyabsurd.com

270 words   Time taken _____

Reading Comprehension

1 Why did the writer choose to write about these four inventions?

   a. They are all dangerous.

   b. They are all very important.

   c. They are all unusual.

   d. They are all expensive.

2 Which invention is best for someone who is gaining weight?

   a. Time Temp Glasses

   b. Alarm Fork

   c. Smell This

   d. Banana Suitcase

3 Which invention is most useful for someone waiting for a train?

   a. Time Temp Glasses

   b. Alarm Fork

   c. Smell This

   d. Banana Suitcase

4 Which invention is best to use before meeting your girlfriend or boyfriend?

   a. Time Temp Glasses

   b. Alarm Fork

   c. Smell This

   d. Banana Suitcase

5 Who might use the Banana Suitcase?

   a. a person who eats bananas only at home

   b. someone who needs to throw away a banana

   c. a person who uses the Alarm Fork

   d. someone who loves bananas and brings lunch to school every day

Fluency Practice

Time yourself as you read through the passage. Try to read as fluently as you can. Record your time in the Reading Rate Chart on page 176. Then answer the questions on the following page.

My Year Abroad

This month in Travelers Corner read about three people's experiences in year-abroad programs:

Mariko Okada — Tokyo

My year abroad in the United States was a truly
5 awesome experience. I'm not a shy person, and I was
very comfortable speaking to everyone, so I got lots of
speaking practice. I also learned lots of interesting things
about American culture. When I got home, my friends
couldn't believe how much I had improved! I hope to go
10 back again in the future.

Carla Fonseca — Rio de Janeiro

I spent last year studying in London. I'm from a small
town, and London is a very big city. Sometimes I felt it was
too big. There were so many people to talk to, but I always
15 felt embarrassed about my English. I missed my family,
and I really missed my two cats. My roommate was always
using our telephone, so I rarely had the chance for a nice
long talk with my parents. I think it was a good experience
for me, but I'm glad to be home!

20 ### Alvin Chen — Hong Kong

Studying in New Zealand was a fun experience for me,
but it was also lots of hard work! I had English classes six
hours a day, five days a week—with lots of homework. I
also kept a journal of my experience. I like to write, and
25 I wrote two or three pages in my journal every day. On
Saturday, my homestay family took me to lots of interesting
places and showed me so many awesome things about New
Zealand culture. I'm definitely glad I went!

270 words   Time taken _____

Reading Comprehension

1 What is true about Mariko, Carla, and Alvin?
   a. They all hope to spend more time abroad in the future.
   b. They all spent a year abroad.
   c. They all speak English very well.
   d. They all worked very hard.

2 Who was very comfortable speaking English?
   a. Mariko
   b. Carla
   c. Alvin
   d. all of the above

3 Why did Carla feel embarrassed?
   a. She missed her cats.
   b. She couldn't speak English well.
   c. London was too big.
   d. Her roommate was using the telephone.

4 Which of these problems is not mentioned by Carla?
   a. She missed her cats.
   b. She couldn't talk on the telephone for a long time.
   c. She missed her cats.
   d. She had too much homework.

5 Which of these activities is not mentioned by Alvin?
   a. homework
   b. speaking practice
   c. journal writing
   d. going to interesting places

music

food

books

clothes

transportation

Getting Ready

Discuss the following questions with a partner.

1 Do you like to spend money? What do you spend it on?
2 How much money do you spend each week on the things in the pictures above?
3 Do you sometimes spend too much money? How does it happen?
4 What are some good ways to be careful with money?

Chapter 1: A Student Budget

A Look at the expenses on the Student Budget Form below. About how much do students in your country pay for those things? What other expenses do university students have?

STUDENT BUDGET WORKSHEET (one year)

Write income[1] and expense[2] information as correctly as possible for one year. If your expenses are more than your inacome, you will need to cut your expenses or to increase your income.

Expenses		Income	
Tuition[3]	$ 18,000	Money from parents	$20,000
Books and supplies	$ 900	Part-time[4] work	$ 5,700
Housing and food	$ 4,010	Your money	$ 0
Phone, cable TV, Internet	$ 640	Other:	$ 100
Clothing	$ 800	Total Income	$ 25,800
Entertainment[5] and personal	$ 1,220		
Transportation	$ 1,460		
Other:	$ 500		
Total Expenses	$ 27,530		

[1]**income** money that comes to you
[2]**expenses** things you spend money on
[3]**tuition** money used to pay for teaching
[4]**part-time** less than 40 hours a week
[5]**entertainment** things you do for fun

B Look at the Income column of the form. What are other ways students get money? Discuss your answers with a partner.

When we "skim" we read over the text quickly. We don't need to read every word, or look up words we do not understand. We do notice key words that are repeated. We skim to get the general idea of the reading passage. Skimming is one way to look for the main ideas in a reading.

A Look at this list of key words that are repeated in the article on the next page. Then scan the article to find them. How many times can you find each one?

1 pay _____ **2** cost _____ **3** money _____

B Skim the article on the next page again. Read only the title, the first paragraph, the first sentence of the middle paragraphs, and the last paragraph. Don't worry about words you don't know. Then complete the sentence below.

The main idea of this reading is _____.
1 the high cost of a university education
2 how to pay for a university education
3 living on a student budget

C Read through the article again and answer the questions that follow.

Student Life 101

A Student Budget

College is an exciting time to learn and to make friends that will last a lifetime. Many students do not like to **worry** about money, and they would rather not think about it. But, it doesn't matter whether a student's parents pay for everything, or whether the student works part-time to help pay for his or her **education**. All students can get into money trouble if they're not careful.

The cost of a college education can be quite expensive. In English-speaking countries, the **average** cost per student per year is well over US$10,000. Students must also pay for books, paper, pens, etc. These can cost $500 to $1,000 per year. Students who live in university housing pay thousands more per year for room and board.[1] Add money for clothes, travel, and other **personal expenses**, and the average cost of one year at a university can be $20,000 to $30,000 or more.

Students need to spend their money carefully. At most universities, advisors[2] can give students **advice** on how to budget their money. They suggest this: at the start of a school semester, write down your income; for example, money you will get from your family or a part-time job. Then, **list** all of your expenses. Put your expenses into two groups: those that change (food, phone, books, travel), and those that will stay the same (tuition, room and board). Add together all of your expenses. Are they more than your income? Do you have enough money, or do you need more?

Learning not to spend more money than you have is not always easy. But for many, it is easier than **borrowing** money from family or friends.

[1] **room and board** cost of a place to stay and meals
[2] **advisors** people who offer helpful ideas to others

Reading Comprehension:
Check Your Understanding

A Decide if the following statements about the reading are true (*T*) or false (*F*). If you check (✓) false, correct the statement to make it true.

	T	F
1 Very few students can get into money trouble.		
2 Most universities have advisors who can help students to budget their money.		
3 If their expenses are more than their income, students must borrow more money.		
4 Learning not to spend more money than you have is very easy.		

B The statements below are about the reading. Choose the correct answer to complete each one.

1 The average cost of a student's books, paper, pens, and other supplies is _____.
   a. $10,000 per year   **b.** $20,000 per year   **c.** $500 to $1,000 per year
2 Students who live in university housing pay thousands more per year for _____.
   a. room and board   **b.** travel   **c.** clothes
3 Expenses that change include _____.
   a. tuition   **b.** room and board   **c.** travel
4 Expenses that stay the same include _____.
   a. clothes   **b.** phone   **c.** tuition

Critical Thinking

C Discuss these questions with your partner.
   1 What are some ways that students can get into money trouble?
   2 The reading says that for many people it is easier to save money than to borrow it from family or friends. Do you agree with this? Why or why not?

Vocabulary Comprehension:
Word Definitions

A Look at the list of words and phrases from the reading. Match each one with a definition on the right.

1 expenses _____
2 education _____
3 list _____
4 borrow _____
5 worry _____
6 average _____
7 personal _____
8 advice _____

a. about one person, not everyone
b. to ask someone to give you money which you will pay back later
c. helpful ideas
d. usual, normal
e. to write down a series of items in a column
f. things you spend money on
g. learning
h. to think too much about things you are afraid about and don't want to happen

B Now complete the sentences using the vocabulary from A. Be sure to use the correct form of the word.

1 My friend _____ $1,500 from me three weeks ago. He said he would pay me back last week, so now I'm really starting to _____.

2 Sometimes it's easier to get a good job if you got your _____ at a good university.

3 It's important to listen to the _____ that older people give you if you want to improve.

4 The school Mark goes to isn't really awesome, but it isn't so bad. It's _____.

A Match each word in the box with a word in the list below that means the opposite.

> expense   inhale   exclude   import   introverted

1 export   _____
2 exhale   _____
3 income   _____
4 include   _____
5 extroverted   _____

B Now choose the correct words from A to match the definitions below.

1 to bring things into a country _____
2 to breathe in _____
3 to leave out _____
4 money that you make _____
5 shy, quiet _____

C Now use the correct words from A to complete the following sentences. Be sure to use the correct form of the word.

1 It is harmful to _____ cigarette smoke.
2 The lunches that our school serves _____ many healthy foods.
3 Taking a vacation abroad was a very big _____. I could hardly pay for it.
4 Hailey isn't shy and quiet. She's quite _____, and is always telling jokes.
5 That company _____ its excellent cars all around the world.

Vocabulary Skill:
The Prefixes *in-* and *ex-*

The prefixes "in-" (or "im-") and "ex-" can often have opposite meanings. "In-" and "im-" often mean "inside" or "into" while "ex-" often means "out" or "away." For example, "income" means money that comes to you; an "expense" is something that makes you spend money, or takes money away.

Chapter 2: My Money

A Answer the questions.

1 Do you sometimes lose sleep thinking about money?
   a. yes   **b.** no

2 How often do you need to borrow money?
   a. often   **b.** sometimes   **c.** never

3 Do you always pay back any money you owe on time?
   a. Yes, always.   **b.** Well, usually.   **c.** No, not always.

4 When you buy something, do you check prices at more than one store before buying it?
   a. No, it takes too much time. I just buy what I need whatever the price.
   b. I sometimes go to other stores if the price seems high.
   c. I always check prices in more than one store.

5 How much money are you saving for the future?
   a. a lot   **b.** some   **c.** almost none

B Discuss your answers with a partner.

Reading Skill:

Identifying Supporting Details

When we identify supporting details, we read carefully for the details that support a main point. Paragraphs are often organized around a main point in the first sentence, and the details that support this point follow in the paragraph. In this reading, Lisa gives details that support her answers to Young Min's questions.

A Scan the article on the next page to find Young Min's question about how Lisa spends her money. Find five supporting details in her answer.

1 _____   4 _____
2 _____   5 _____
3 _____

B Scan the article to find Young Min's question about how Lisa saves money. Find four details supporting her answer.

1 _____
2 _____
3 _____
4 _____

C Read through the article and answer the questions that follow.

http://www.ACTIVEmoneyspot.com

My Money

In this week's *Students Around the World*, Young Min Kim interviews an American university student, Lisa Conroy. They talk about living on a student budget.

Young Min: Thanks for talking with me today, Lisa. Tell us a little about yourself. 5

Lisa: Well, I'm twenty-one, and I'm a junior[1] at a university in Chicago.

Young Min: How are you paying for your college education?

Lisa: My expenses for every semester[2] are almost $15,000. At the start of each semester my parents pay the $10,000 tuition. I also get $2,000 from my college. I have to **earn** the rest myself. 10

Young Min: How do you do that? 15

Lisa: I have a part-time job at a hotel. I work about twenty hours a week, and earn $400. After **taxes**, I make about $320.

Young Min: How do you spend that money?

Lisa: It helps to pay for my **rent** and meals at college. It also pays for things like my cell phone, books, **transportation**, and clothes. 20

Young Min: You don't have much money for fun, do you?

Lisa: That's true! My mother advised me to **stick to** my budget carefully so I don't have to borrow. I don't like to **owe** people money. I hardly ever go to the movies. My roommates and I usually rent movies and **split** the cost, so it's cheaper. 25

Young Min: How else do you save money?

Lisa: I don't go to restaurants. I cook with my roommates so it's cheaper to eat. I try to walk or ride my bicycle to college. Oh, and I buy a lot of my clothes at **second-hand** stores. You can find some very cheap, nice clothes in those stores. 30

[1]**junior** In four-year university programs, a first-year student is called a *freshman*, a second-year student is called a *sophomore*, a third-year student is called a *junior*, and a fourth-year student is called a *senior*.

[2]**semester** part of the school year, usually half

Reading Comprehension:

Check Your Understanding

A **How much do you remember from the reading? Choose the best answer to complete each statement below.**

1 Lisa's expenses every semester are almost _____.
   a. $2,000   **b.** $10,000   **c.** $15,000
2 Lisa has a part-time job at a _____.
   a. restaurant   **b.** theater   **c.** hotel
3 Lisa's _____ advised her to stick to her budget carefully.
   a. advisor   **b.** teacher   **c.** mother
4 Lisa tries to stick to a budget so she will not have to _____.
   a. buy cheap clothes   **b.** ride her bicycle   **c.** borrow money

B **Decide if the following statements about the reading are true (*T*) or false (*F*). If you check (✓) false, correct the statement to make it true.**

	T	F
1 Lisa is a second-year university student.		
2 Lisa has lots of money for fun.		
3 Lisa doesn't like to owe people money.		
4 Lisa usually shops for clothes in second-hand stores.		

Critical Thinking

C **Discuss these questions with your partner.**

1 What kind of person do you think Lisa is? Is she similar to you or different from you?
2 Do you buy your clothes in second-hand stores? What other things can students buy second-hand to save money?

Vocabulary Comprehension:

Words in Context

A **The words in *italics* are vocabulary items from the reading. Read each question or statement and choose the correct answer.**

1 If you *earn* money, you _____.
   a. work for it   **b.** receive it as a gift
2 If you *owe* someone money it means _____.
   a. you borrowed money and need to pay it back
   b. you give them money for a short time
3 If you *rent* something, does it belong to you?
   a. yes   **b.** no
4 When you *split* the cost of something with a friend, _____.
   a. your friend pays   **b.** you both pay

5 *Tax* money goes to support _____.
   a. your entertainment   **b.** your country
6 For *transportation* I can choose between _____.
   a. the bus or the subway   **b.** the cafeteria or a restaurant
7 Melissa really *sticks to* her budget, so _____.
   a. she doesn't have much money for fun
   b. she can spend as much as she wants
8 You can save a lot of money in *second-hand* _____ stores.
   a. computer   **b.** food

B Now complete the sentences below using the vocabulary from A. Be sure
to use the correct form of the word.

1 I really _____ $600 a week, but I only take home $500, because
  I have to pay $100 in _____.
2 The average student doesn't have a car. Most use public _____
  such as the subway.
3 Many people borrow money to pay for their university education, and they
  often still _____ money to the bank many years later.
4 My expenses aren't bad because some are _____ with my
  roommates. For example, every month we pay the _____ together.

A The following words are all used to talk about money. Some are used to talk
about money coming in to you; others are used to talk about money going
out. Write each word on the correct line below.

expense	borrow	income	earn	buy
lend	owe	rent	pay	spend

1 Money coming in: _____
2 Money going out: _____

B Complete the sentences using the correct words from A. Be sure to use
the correct form of each word.

1 I need to _____ some money from the bank to buy a new
  washing machine.
2 My brother wants me to _____ him some money.
  He's _____ all his money on CDs!
3 I think we have to _____ an air conditioner. The temperature hit
  38 degrees today. But it's such a big _____.
4 How much tax do you pay on your _____ in an average year?
5 Could I ask you a personal question? How much do you pay each month
  in _____ on this apartment?

**Vocabulary
Skill:**

Organizing
Vocabulary: Words
Relating to Money

When you learn
new vocabulary,
it can help you to
think about other
words that are
used to talk about
the same topic.
We can divide
these words into
groups to help us
remember them
better.

Real Life Skill:
Creating a Personal Budget

A personal budget can help you to spend your money more carefully. But, most people don't create a personal budget because they think it is difficult. Actually, creating a personal budget can be quite simple and fun. With a little practice, anyone can improve their budgeting skills.

A Create a personal monthly budget. Follow the steps below.

Step 1: Write your income for one month.

> Monthly income: $1,500

Step 2: Write down all the expenses that you have to spend money on each month. Think about how much you spend each month on them. Write down how much you spend on each and add the numbers.

> 1. Rent...................................$800
> 2. Food..................................$200
> 3. Clothes.............................$100
> 4. Heat &
>   Electricity.........................$50
>   Necessary Expenses............$1,150

Step 3: Now write down how much you spend on other things. Add the numbers.

> 1. Restaurants.........................$150
> 2. Movies................................$60
> 3. Music CDs...........................$100
>   Other Expenses....................$310

Step 4: Add all your expenses together and subtract them from your income. Then you'll see how much extra money you have every month.

> 1. Income..............................$1,500
> 2. Expenses...........................$1,460
>   Extra Money!.......................$40

B **Internet Challenge: Use the search words "student," "budget," and "worksheet" to find student budget worksheets online. Use your dictionary to look up words you don't know. Print out or copy the worksheet and share it with a group of classmates.**

What Do You Think?

1 What are some ways that parents can teach their children to spend money carefully?
2 What are some popular ways for students to make extra money?
3 What are some easy ways to spend too much money?
4 If you have extra money at the end of the month, what is the best thing to do with it?

Our Modern Lifestyle

Technology Complaints

	Agree	Disagree

Cell Phones

1 It makes me angry when people talk loudly on their cell phones in public places. I don't want to hear their conversations

2 People shouldn't drive and talk on a cell phone at the same time. It's really dangerous.

3 I often lose my cell phone.

4 Cell phones are too expensive to use.

5 _____

The Internet

1 People shouldn't try to get music from the Internet without paying for it.

2 I don't buy things on the Internet because I'm afraid I will never receive anything.

3 It worries me that people are watching me when I e-mail or use the Internet.

4 I think people shouldn't put other people's information or pictures on the Internet without asking them first.

5 _____

Getting Ready

Discuss the following questions with a partner.

1 Look at the technology complaints in the chart above. Check (✓) *Agree* or *Disagree* for each one.

2 Write one more complaint about cell phones and one about the Internet in the chart.

3 Compare and explain your answers with a partner. Does your partner agree with your complaints?

Chapter 1: Cell Phone Etiquette

Before You Read:
Using Cell Phones

A Scan the letter on the next page to find the answers to the following questions.

1. Who was this letter sent to? _____
2. Who sent this letter? _____
3. What is the Sunday Globe? _____
4. Amber Jala is probably _____.
   a. an employee at a cell phone company
   b. a regular newspaper reader
   c. a university advisor
5. Which paragraph is about personal space?
   a. the first   b. the second   c. the third
6. Which paragraph is about loudness?
   a. the second   b. the third   c. the fourth
7. Which paragraph is about doing two things at the same time?
   a. the first   b. the third   c. the fourth

B Discuss your answers with a partner.

Reading Skill:
Identifying Transition Words

It is very important to know about transition words and how they show the relationship between ideas. A good understanding of transition words can improve our understanding and reading speed.

A Scan the letter on the next page to find these transition words. Circle them.

thus	likewise	for instance	furthermore
in fact	additionally	that's why	on the other hand

B How are the transition words used? Write them on the line beside their use.

to show a result (2)	_____
to give more information (3)	_____
to show that something is the same	_____
to show that something is different	_____
to give examples	_____

C Read through the letter again and answer the questions that follow.

Cell Phone Etiquette

Dear Sunday Globe:

I am writing to you about your article in last Sunday's newspaper, "Cell Phones Make Life Easier." You did an excellent job explaining the good points of cell phones; they're **convenient**, we feel safer always being able to call someone, and they are very helpful in business. On the other hand, 5 you didn't talk about their bad points at all. Thus, I hope you'll let me give your readers some advice on cell phone etiquette.

The first point I'd like to **address** is loudness. When talking face to face in public, you wouldn't shout. Likewise, don't shout when you talk on your cell phone in public. In fact, the microphones in cell phones are so 10 **sensitive** that you can be heard even if you speak quietly. Furthermore, keep your ringer nice and quiet—and don't let it ring in meetings, at the movies, etc.

Another point that needs to be made has to do with personal space. I think it is very **impolite** to make calls in small spaces or crowded rooms. 15 This makes others uncomfortable and forces them to listen to your personal business. Additionally, it stops many face-to-face conversations from ever beginning; that's why I never use my cell phone within three meters of other people except in **emergencies**, and only after asking 20 **permission**.

Lastly, let me draw your readers' **attention** to the dangers of doing two things at the same time. For instance, cell phones and driving are a bad **combination**. Pay attention to the road! Likewise, cell phones can cause you to neglect good friends. Give friends who are with you your full 25 attention. Turn off your cell phone and enjoy their company!

Sincerely,

Amber Jala

Amber Jala

Reading Comprehension:

Check Your Understanding

A How much do you remember about the reading? Choose the best answer for each question or statement below.

1 Why did Amber decide to write this letter?
   a. She wanted to talk about the good points of cell phones.
   b. She liked the article in the *Sunday Globe* about cell phones.
   c. She thought the bad points of cell phones weren't included in the article.

2 When talking on a cell phone or face to face, _____.
   a. it's not necessary to speak very loudly
   b. the microphone is sensitive enough to hear
   c. you should speak very quietly

3 Amber thinks that making a phone call in a crowded elevator is _____.
   a. sensitive   **b.** an emergency   **c.** impolite

4 Amber thinks that if you talk on your cell phone while doing something else, _____.
   a. you might not pay attention to what you're doing
   b. your friends will enjoy being with you more
   c. you will save a lot of time

B Write the number of the paragraph (1–4) that best matches each piece of advice.

1 Never make a call in a car full of people. ____
2 Remember to speak normally. ____
3 Don't talk on your phone and pay for something at the same time. ____
4 Keep your ringer quiet. ____

Critical Thinking

C Discuss these questions with your partner.

1 Do you always follow Amber's rules of cell phone etiquette? Explain.
2 Think of specific examples of why cell phones are convenient.
3 When could having a cell phone make someone feel safer?

Vocabulary Comprehension:

Odd Word Out

A For each group, circle the word that does not belong. The words in *italics* are vocabulary items from the reading.

1	*address*	speak about	listen
2	notice	*attention*	kindness
3	mix	experience	*combination*
4	*convenient*	awesome	excellent
5	problem	*emergency*	joke
6	support	help	*permission*
7	*impolite*	sweet	nice
8	understanding	*sensitive*	loud

B Now complete the sentences below using the words in *italics* from A.

1 It is very _____ to borrow something from someone without asking for _____ first.
2 That bird has very _____ eyes. I hardly moved my head, but it saw me.
3 Students! Stop talking now and please give me your _____.
4 For me, the subway is the most _____ form of transportation. One comes every ten minutes during the day.

A Look at this chart of different relationships between ideas, and the transition words that show the relationships.

Relationship	Transition Words
contrast	on the other hand; however
show a result	thus; therefore; that's why
add	in addition; furthermore; in fact
compare	likewise; similarly
give examples	for example; for instance

Transition words show the relationship between ideas. Knowing them and their uses makes reading much easier. They can also help you to write more interesting sentences.

B Use transition words from A to complete these sentences.

1 That country has many unusual customs; _____, when people meet someone, they hit the person on the head.
2 I am embarrassed about them putting my picture in the newspaper without asking my permission; _____ I have written a letter to the newspaper asking them to apologize.
3 I always write in my travel journal when I am on vacation; _____, my sister has a notebook in which she writes down everything we do on vacation.
4 I spend all the money I earn very quickly and never save any; _____, my brother sticks to a budget and saves a lot of money every month.
5 I've borrowed more money than I can pay back. I owe $100 to Sergio, $50 to Simon, $75 to Ryoko, and $500 for the rent; _____, I owe $700 in income taxes this year!
6 I've been wearing second-hand clothes all my life and I don't want to anymore; _____, I'm going shopping for all new clothes this weekend!
7 I'm naturally a curious person; _____, my mother is always asking questions and wants to know everything.

Chapter 2: Moblogging

Before You Read:
Blogs

A *Blogs* are a kind of website. People who have blogs often put or *post* new information on them. The newest information is posted at the top of the page.

1 Have you ever visited a blog?
2 Look at this list of different topics of blogs. Circle the topics you would be interested in reading about.

Topics of Blogs		
personal	games	sports
business	photos	movies
science	experiences	music

B Discuss your answers with a partner. Together, think of three more topics for blogs.

Reading Skill:
Making Inferences

When we make inferences, we look at some information in a reading passage and we try to get more meaning from it. Making inferences is important because sometimes the writer doesn't give us all the meaning. By making inferences we can be active readers and understand more.

A Scan the article on the next page to find the words in *italics* below. Read the area around the words and make inferences about the meaning. Choose the best answer to complete each statement.

1 In line 6, *post* probably means _____.
   a. sell   **b.** put   **c.** send
2 In line 11, *reporter* probably means _____.
   a. a person whose job is to tell us the news
   b. a student who writes reports
   c. a person who makes movies
3 In line 16, *broadcast* probably means _____.
   a. talked about by many people
   b. put on a television news show
   c. posted on the Internet for people to read about
4 In line 25, *but she refused to clean it up, became angry, and left,* the woman probably became angry because _____.
   a. she didn't like her dog
   b. she didn't want to clean up the mess
   c. she didn't want her picture on the Internet
5 In line 30, *One idea from Japan may help*, the new idea is helpful because _____.
   a. everyone will know when a cell phone picture is taken
   b. pictures will be taken faster than before with camera phones
   c. everyone will ask permission before taking pictures

B Read through the article again and answer the questions that follow.

Moblogging

Moblog is a combination of two words. The first word is *mobile*, which means a *mobile camera phone* or *camera*. The second word is *blog*, a website for **posting** words and pictures. **Typically**, mobloggers are people who take photos or videos with their phones and post them on the Internet. Moblogging has caused a lot of excitement. It has also caused a lot of **concern**.

5

With a picture phone and a moblog, anyone can be a reporter. Moblogging first got the world's attention during a terrorist attack on four London buses. People were

10

posting photos on the Internet many minutes before real reporters could get there. Similarly, information about car **accidents** has been **broadcast** right away.

15

Moblogging is done just for fun, too. Posted on some moblogs you can find photos of friends making funny faces, photos from people traveling, and photos of new babies. Other fun moblogs might be spotting famous people, pictures of food in restaurants, or new clothes.

20

However, moblogs can be dangerous, too. Not long ago in Korea, a woman's dog made a mess on the train, but she **refused** to clean it up, became angry, and left. Her picture was taken and posted on the Internet, **along with** the story of what she did. People all around the country were angry with her. **Imagine** how she felt! Moblogging can be wonderful, but it's really impolite to post another person's picture on the Internet without asking permission. One idea from Japan may help: people can no longer quietly take pictures with their cell phones. Japanese cell phones "click" like a real camera when you take a picture.

25

30

Reading Comprehension:
Check Your Understanding

A Answer these questions about the reading.

1 Moblog is a combination of which two words?

_____

2 Moblogging first caught the world's attention during a terrorist attack on what?

_____

3 Give two examples of photos that might be found on a fun moblog.

_____

4 How did people all around the country feel about the woman who refused to clean up after her dog?

_____

B Decide if the following statements about the reading are true (*T*), false (*F*), or if the information is not given (*NG*). If you check (✓) false, correct the statement to make it true.

	T	F	NG
1 Mobloggers can post news on the Internet faster than real reporters.			
2 Moblogs can be dangerous.			
3 It isn't very expensive to start a moblog.			
4 Japanese cell phones are completely quiet.			

Critical Thinking

C Discuss these questions with your partner.
1 What is it about moblogging that has caused people some concern?
2 How did the Korean dog owner probably feel after her picture and story was posted on the Internet?

Vocabulary Comprehension:
Word Definitions

A Look at the list of words from the reading. Match each word with a definition on the right.

1 accident _____
2 along with _____
3 post _____
4 broadcast _____
5 concern _____
6 imagine _____
7 refuse _____
8 typically _____

a. to send out (like news) on TV or on the Internet
b. to think in a creative way
c. to put on the Internet
d. together with
e. to say "No"
f. usually
g. cars hitting each other; a big mistake
h. worry or serious thinking

B **Now complete the sentences below using words from A. Be sure to use the correct form of the word.**

1 I asked my father to split the bill with me, but he _____.
He always wants to pay for me.

2 _____, I come to school _____ my brother. But,
he's sick today.

3 Did you see the news about the car _____? It was _____
on my friend's blog.

4 Can you _____ how different the world will be in 200 years?

A **Create a word web about moblogging. Use words in the box and other words from this chapter. Explain your diagram to a partner.**

**Vocabulary
Skill:**
Word Webs

A helpful way to
remember new
vocabulary is to
create a "word
web." Word webs
can help you
to link the new
words you have
learned together,
or to vocabulary
you already know.

moblog	website	Internet	celebrities
camera phone	broadcast	post	education
photos	text	topics	
opinions	food	blog	

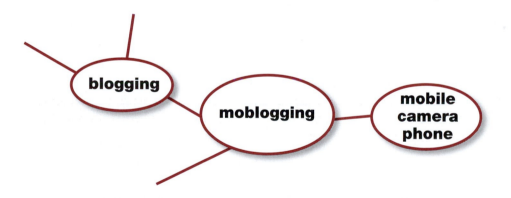

B **Now try making a word web using words you find in another chapter. See how many branches and words you can add. Share your ideas with a partner.**

Real Life Skill:
Reading Blogs

In this chapter you learned that blogs are a kind of website. There are many different types of blogs with lots of different information, but in some ways blogs are also much the same. They all have *posts*. Posts are like short reading passages on a blog. Posts nearly always have a date and a title. Remember, in a typical blog, the newest post is on top.

A On your computer, follow these steps to collect some information about a blog.

1 Search the Internet using the search words "chess blog."
2 Click on one of the chess blogs you found.
3 What is the name of the blog? _____
4 What is the title of the newest post? _____
5 What is the date of the newest post? _____

B Now do four more Internet searches to fill in the information in the chart. Then do two more searches using your own Internet search words.

Internet search words	The name of the blog	The title of the newest post	The date of the newest post
soccer blog			
movie blog			
music blog			
English blog			

C Tell your partner about any interesting blogs you found.

What Do You Think?

1 Do you think that new technologies are making our lives better? If yes, in what ways? If no, why not?
2 Some people say there is too much information in the world today. Do you agree or disagree? Explain your answer.
3 Do you have a personal web page or blog? If yes, describe it. If no, would you like to have one?

The Olympics

Getting Ready

Discuss the following questions with a partner.

1 Do you know the names of the Olympic events in the pictures?
2 How many other Olympic events can you name?
3 What are the names of some cities where the Olympic Games have been held?
4 Where will the next Olympic Games be held?

Chapter 1: Choosing the Olympic City

A **For a city hoping to become an Olympic host city, four of these eight points need to be true. Check (✓) those four points.**

1 ❑ The city must have a well-run public transportation system.
2 ❑ The city must have an excellent university.
3 ❑ There must be at least one international airport in the area.
4 ❑ The city must be ready for 100,000 visitors.
5 ❑ All rude people must leave the city.
6 ❑ Restaurants in the city must not serve junk food.
7 ❑ The city must have experience hosting other very big events.
8 ❑ The people of the city must have interesting customs.

B **Discuss your answers, and the following questions, with a partner.**

1 What other points are important for an Olympic host city?
2 What are the first steps a city should take to become an Olympic host city?

In some readings, events appear in the order that they happen. Dates, times, and numbers help to show the order. Sequence words like *first*, *then*, *next*, *later*, *after*, and *finally* also help us to know the order of events.

A **Scan the reading on the next page to put the events on the Time Line below in the correct order (1–10).**

Olympic Host City Application Time Line

4	About one year later, the IOC selects several cities on the basis of government support, safety, hotels, transportation, etc.
	After they are selected, the cities must pay a fee of around US$500,000 if they want to continue the application process.
	After viewing the cities, they write reports about them for the IOC.
	Finally, two years after the process began, the IOC holds a special meeting.
	After that, the application process is explained to the candidates at a meeting.
	First, the IOC invites national Olympic committees to apply to host the Games.
	In the first step of Phase II, the IOC gives candidate cities an application process guide and list of questions.
	Next, the cities must submit the candidature file.
8	Several months later, people from the IOC take a trip to the candidate cities.
1	The IOC starts the application process nine years before the Olympic Games.

B **Circle any words or numbers in the sentences that can help you understand the sequence. Compare your answers with a partner.**

C **Read through the passage again and answer the questions that follow.**

Choosing the Olympic City

Every two years, the International Olympic Committee (IOC) selects a city to host the Olympic Games. It's always very exciting. Since the year 2000, Sydney, Salt Lake City, Athens, Beijing, Torino, London, and Vancouver have all been chosen to host the Olympic Games. The IOC makes this decision very carefully. The application process is very long, slow, and difficult. Cities that **apply** need to work very hard. 5

Phase I—Applicant Cities

The IOC starts the application **process** nine years before the Olympic Games. First, the IOC invites national Olympic committees to apply to host the Games. The IOC then holds a meeting for people from the national Olympic 10 committees of cities that have decided to apply. At the meeting, the IOC explains the application requirements to the cities. About one year later, the IOC **selects** several cities on the basis of **government** support, safety, hotels, transportation, etc. After they are selected, the cities are **required** to pay a fee[1] of around US$500,000 if they want to continue the application process. 15 Cities that decide to continue are then called *candidate cities*.

Phase II—Candidate Cities

In the first step of Phase II, the IOC gives candidate cities an application process **guide** and list of questions. Candidate cities must first answer the questions. Next, the cities must **submit** the *candidature file*. This file explains 20 in detail the city's plans to host the Olympic Games. The IOC reads the candidature file. Several months later, people from the IOC take a trip to the candidate cities. After viewing the cities, they write reports about them for the IOC. Finally, two years after the process began, the IOC holds a special meeting. It is there that they **announce** their selection for host city, seven 25 years before the Olympic Games will begin.

[1]**fee** money paid for a service

Reading Comprehension:
Check Your Understanding

A How much do you remember from the reading? Choose the best answer to complete each statement below.

1 The host city application process begins _____ years before the start of the Olympic Games.
   a. five   **b.** seven   **c.** nine

2 The IOC is interested in the government support, hotels, and _____ of applicant cities.
   a. transportation   **b.** beauty   **c.** restaurants

3 The candidature file explains in detail _____.
   a. events of the Olympic Games
   b. the Olympic host city application process
   c. plans for hosting the Olympic Games

4 The IOC tells everyone the name of the host city _____.
   a. in the host city
   b. at a special meeting
   c. during the Olympic Games

B Do these steps take place in Phase I or in Phase II? Write I or II beside each step.

_____ Cities submit the candidature file.
_____ The IOC invites cities to apply to host the games.
_____ People from the IOC visit the candidate city.
_____ Cities pay a high fee.

Critical Thinking

C Discuss these questions with your partner.

1 What city would you suggest for hosting a future summer Olympic Games? What about a future winter Olympic Games? Explain your reasons.

2 Do you think that the way Olympic host cities are chosen is good? Is there any way it could be improved?

Vocabulary Comprehension:
Words in Context

A The words in *italics* are vocabulary items from the reading. Read each question or statement and choose the best answer.

1 When you *announce* some news, you _____.
   a. tell it to people   **b.** study it carefully

2 A *government* makes decisions for _____.
   a. a country   **b.** a company

3 Many machines come with a *guide* that tells us _____.
   a. how they were made   **b.** how to use them

4 People *apply* _____.
   a. for jobs and to colleges   **b.** to make friends and dinner

5 A *process* is an activity that is usually _____.
   a. quickly finished   **b.** long and has a number of steps

6 Teachers *require* most students _____.
   a. to do homework   **b.** to get a job
7 To *select* something means _____.
   a. to clean it   **b.** to choose it
8 If you *submit* a paper to someone, you _____.
   a. give it to them   **b.** explain it to them

B Answer these questions. Share your ideas with a partner.

1 What are some things that students *require*?
_____

2 Where are some *government* buildings located?
_____

3 What are some good places to *apply* for a job?
_____

4 What do universities want to know when they *select* new students?
_____

A Add the suffix *-ment* to the verbs in the box to form nouns. Use the nouns to complete the sentences below.

> announce   embarrass   encourage   require
> entertain   govern   improve

1 Did you hear that important _____? It said that there is a fire in the building and we need to get out quickly!
2 The _____ of the United States is located in Washington, D.C.
3 I was really nervous about speaking in front of the class, but your words of _____ have made me feel much better.
4 Luis started wearing a necktie this week. I think it is such an _____ in the way he looks.
5 My girlfriend posted an ugly picture of me on the Internet. It was really an _____ for me!
6 Excuse me, Mr. Silva. What are the _____ for this course? Will there be many tests and homework?
7 The _____ at our party will include music, dancing, and games.

B Write the noun form of each of these verbs. Only four of them use the suffix *-ment.* Use your dictionary to help you.

1 arrange _____
2 agree _____
3 imagine _____
4 refuse _____
5 argue _____
6 judge _____
7 select _____
8 submit _____

Vocabulary Skill:
The Suffix *-ment*

One of the uses of the suffix "-ment" is to change certain verbs into nouns. When we add the suffix "-ment" to the verb "embarrass," the verb becomes the noun "embarrassment."

Chapter 2: Unusual Olympic Sports

Before You Read:
Unusual Sports

A Answer the following questions.

1 Look at this list of Olympic events that some people think are unusual.
Do you agree? Circle the ones that you know.

> • archery   • tae kwon do   • water polo
> • snowboarding   • equestrian   • synchronized
> • bobsledding   • tug-of-war   swimming
> • canoeing   • fencing

2 One of the events in A used to be an Olympic event, but it isn't anymore.
Which one do you think it is?

3 Now look at the pictures of three unusual Olympic sports on page 75.
Do you agree that these are unusual sports? Why do you think so?

B Discuss your answers with a partner.

Reading Skill:
Reading for Details

When reading for details, we read every word and make sure to understand the meaning. This can be useful for test-taking. We can use scanning to find the part of the reading that has the information we want, and then read for details.

A Read the section on curling in the passage on the next page. Decide if the following statements are true (*T*), false (*F*), or if the information is not given (*NG*). If you check (✓) false, correct the statement to make it true.

		T	F	NG
1	Curling is played on ice.			
2	There are six players all together.			
3	The stones never touch the center of the house			

B Read the section on skeleton racing in the passage on the next page and decide if the following statements are true (*T*), false (*F*), or if the information is not given (*NG*). If you check (✓) false, correct the statement to make it true.

		T	F	NG
1	Skeleton became an Olympic sport in 1938.			
2	The skeleton sled is simple.			
3	Skeleton is a very dangerous sport.			

C Read the passage again and answer the questions that follow.

http://www.ASRsportsnews.com

Unusual Olympic Sports

We interviewed three Olympic competitors in sports you may not have heard of: curling; biathlon; and skeleton.

Curling

Curling is a sport that is played on ice. Two teams of four players each **slide** eight stones along the ice to a colored circle on the ice (called the *house*). The **object** is to place a stone closest to the center of the house. "I started curling very young," Canadian Olympic curler Sammy McCann told us. "My father **managed** a hotel with an ice rink. As soon as the people would leave the ice, my friends and I would get right on and start curling." 5 10

Biathlon

Biathlon has been an Olympic event since 1960. It is a combination of cross-country skiing and shooting. 15

"Biathlon comes from the tradition of **hunting** on skis," said Norwegian biathlon competitor Anne Kristiansen. "In Norway, you can either play soccer or do cross-country skiing; since soccer didn't interest me, I tried skiing. But, skiing was a little boring, until at age eight I tried biathlon. I won my first event at age twelve, and I've stuck to it." 20

Skeleton

The sport of skeleton **racing** first became an Olympic sport in 1928. Skeleton racers slide down an icy course at very high speed on a simple sled. The sled is called a skeleton because early sleds **looked like** human skeletons. 25

"I didn't start skeleton until I was 30," said American skeleton racer Zach Gale. "While driving, my girlfriend and I **took a wrong turn** at Lake Placid, New York. That's where the 1980 Winter Olympics **took place**. They were offering skeleton classes that afternoon. My girlfriend said, 'Why don't we give it a try?' It was fun! I fell in love with it." 30

Reading Comprehension:
Check Your Understanding

A The statements below are about the reading. Complete each one using the correct word or phrase.

1 Sammy McCann started curling when he was _____.
2 Biathlon is a mix of _____ and _____.
3 Before Anne Kristiansen tried biathlon, she thought that skiing was _____.
4 Zach Gale didn't start skeleton racing until he was _____.

B Match each statement with the sport it describes.

1 The object is to place a stone closest to the center of the house _____.
2 It's the fastest of the three events _____.
3 It's been an Olympic event since 1960 _____.
4 It's a team sport _____.

    a. biathlon
    b. curling
    c. skeleton

Critical Thinking

C Discuss these questions with your partner.

1 Why do some people like to do these unusual sports rather than the more usual ones?
2 Zach Gale said that he didn't start skeleton until he was 30. At what age do Olympic athletes usually begin training? How old is too old to be an Olympic athlete?
3 Does your government give support to Olympic athletes? How?

Vocabulary Comprehension:
Word Definitions

A Look at the list of words and phrases from the reading. Match each one with a definition on the right.

1 hunt _____
2 look like _____
3 object _____
4 race _____
5 slide _____
6 take a wrong turn _____
7 take place _____
8 manage _____

a. to seem the same to the eye
b. to take care of (a business)
c. to go left instead of right or right instead of left
d. move on ice
e. a speed competition in running, driving, etc.
f. to find and kill animals
g. goal; the main idea of a game
h. to happen

B Now complete the sentences below using the vocabulary from A. Be sure to use the correct form of the word.

1 It is a very old tradition in parts of Canada for the Inuit people to _____ animals such as whales, seals, and bears.
2 When the skeleton _____ began, the competitors ran with their sleds, jumped on them, and began to _____ down the mountain.

3 Before I cut my hair, people said I _____ my sister.

4 The 2004 Olympic Games _____ in Athens, Greece.

A The following words are all related to sport. Put them into one of the columns below. Can you add any other words to these columns? Share your ideas with a partner.

Vocabulary Skill:

Organizing Vocabulary: Words Relating to Money

court	bat	ring	bicycle	coach
racket	ball	stick	champion	puck
player	competitor	stadium	gloves	club
team	opponent	skates	sled	net
field	rink	velodrome	course	manager

One helpful way to remember new words is to put them into meaningful groups; for example, positive and negative, or people, places, and things. Putting vocabulary in groups like this can help you to remember new words and relate them to other words you know.

Where sport takes place	Sports equipment	Sports people
court	racket	player

B Now complete the following sentences using vocabulary from A. Make sure to use the correct form of the word.

1 There are four _____ on a curling _____.

2 Baseball and football are both played on a _____.

3 You play tennis on a _____ with a _____ and a _____.

4 Boxers wear big _____ and fight in a _____.

5 Speed skating takes place on a _____ and the competitors wear _____.

6 Field hockey and ice hockey are played with _____. In ice hockey there is no ball, instead players use a _____.

Real Life Skill:
Understanding
Punctuation

Punctuation marks—small symbols like , ! ? —are important in text because they help show the meaning of the sentence, and how it should be read. To read and write English well you need to understand how, why, and when punctuation marks are used.

A Find one example of each punctuation mark below in the reading passage on page 75 and circle it. Then match the marks with the descriptions of how they work.

. period	_____
, comma	_____
; semi-colon	_____
: colon	_____
( ) parentheses	_____
? question mark	_____
! exclamation point	_____
" " quotation marks	_____

a. shows what a person said

b. shows the end of a strong or surprising sentence

c. shows the end of a question

d. shows the end of a sentence

e. separates a sentence into different parts

f. separates a sentence, usually before a list

g. shows a separate idea inside a sentence

h. shows that two sentences go together

B Now add punctuation marks to these sentences. Compare your answers with a partner.

1 After the host city was selected work began on the new sports center
2 My father said I am not angry with you
3 I have applied for a job at three companies Monsanto Motorola and Westinghouse
4 She refused to address the problem she didn't have the time
5 Call the police This is an emergency
6 She kept asking me Are you angry
7 I like soccer and I like basketball but I really don't like baseball
8 We had Vietnamese food for dinner it's delicious

What Do You Think?

1 There are many sports and games that are not now part of the Olympic Games. What new events could be added to the Olympic Games?
2 Do you think the Olympic Games are becoming more popular or less popular?
3 Say your opinion about which country's athletes are the best at each of these events: skiing, gymnastics, track and field, swimming, and wrestling.
4 If you could become an Olympic athlete, which event would you participate in?

Fluency Strategy: *KWL*

Readers can ask themselves three questions to improve their reading fluency and comprehension. The letters K, W, and L can be used to remind you of these questions. KWL stands for **K**now, **W**ant, **L**earn.

Know

The first step in KWL is similar to the Survey step in SQ3R (page 41) and the A in the ACTIVE approach (inside front cover). This step will help you prepare yourself before reading.

A Look at the title on the right, taken from the article on the next page. From the title, decide "What is the topic of the passage?"

Money-saving Tips for Students

B Ask yourself, "What do I already know about this topic?" Write down three or four facts that you already know about the topic in the Know column of the table below.

Know	Want	Learn
1.	1.	1.
2.	2.	2.
3.	3.	3.
4.	4.	4.

Want

In the second stage of KWL, ask yourself, "What do I **want** to learn as I read?" By doing this, you are reading with a purpose. This step is similar to the Question step in SQ3R.

A Ask yourself what you want to learn as you read "Money-saving Tips for Students." Write down two or three things you hope to learn in the **Want** column above.

B Before going on to the L in KWL, read the passage "Money-saving Tips for Students" on the next page.

Money-saving Tips for Students

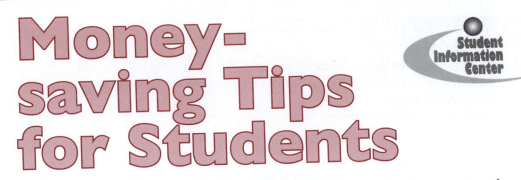

Student Information Center

One problem that most university students understand is not having enough money. Here are some money-saving tips for students we think will help.

Tip 1: Every month, make a list of your expenses in a notebook. Write down what you spend money on, and when you spend it. Also, write down the income you get
5   each month. Doing this will help you make better decisions about when to spend— and when not to spend.

Tip 2: If you have the time, getting a job is, of course, one of the best ways to earn money. But even better is getting a job in a restaurant. Some restaurants give food to their workers, so
10   you won't need to worry about paying for meals.

Tip 3: Buy secondhand textbooks whenever you can. When you buy them from another student, you won't even have to pay tax. Many students sell lots of other things when they leave. Make sure to look around for lists of used things for
15   sale at your university, and shop at secondhand stores if you can.

Tip 4: Eating in restaurants can be very expensive. You can save money by eating at home with family or by eating breakfast, lunch, or dinner with your roommates and splitting
20   the cost.

Tip 5: You can spend less money on transportation if you buy a bus or train pass. This can save you 30 percent or more. Cars are a big expense, so if you live on the university
25   campus, leave the car at your parents' home.

Learn

Now that you have finished reading, ask yourself, "What did I **learn** while reading?" Did you learn what you wanted to? This step is similar to the Review and Recite stages of SQ3R (page 43).

A Write down three or four things you learned from "Money-saving Tips for Students" in the **Learn** column of the chart on page 79.

B Now test how much you learned from the passage by answering these questions.

1 The main idea of this reading is to
   a. explain why university students often don't have enough money.
   b. give university students advice on saving money.
   c. show university students how to make a budget.
   d. make sure university students don't borrow money.

2 Which two tips talk about saving money on food?
   a. Tips 1 and 3
   b. Tips 2 and 4
   c. Tips 3 and 5
   d. Tips 1 and 5

3 When is it not necessary to pay tax?
   a. when you buy books at a bookstore
   b. when you buy things at a secondhand store
   c. when you buy used textbooks from another student
   d. when you leave your car at your parents' home

4 Why do students probably sell things when they leave?
   a. They want to start a new business.
   b. They don't want to take too much with them.
   c. They need to help other students.
   d. They don't want to pay tax.

5 Who could Tip 5 help?
   a. a student with a car living at his or her parents' home
   b. a student with a car living on a university campus in a city with buses and trains
   c. a student without a car living on a big-city university campus
   d. a student without a car living at his or her parents' home

6 Which piece of advice is not in the reading?
   a. You should make a list of all your expenses.
   b. You should look for lists of used things for sale.
   c. You should buy a bus or train pass.
   d. You should borrow money from your parents.

Self Check

Write a short answer to each of the following questions.

1. Have you ever used the KWL method before?

   Yes   No   I'm not sure.

2. Do you think KWL is helpful? Why or why not?

   _____

   _____

3. How can you practice KWL in your reading outside
   of English class?

   _____

   _____

4. When you are reading, do you find yourself having to translate?
   If yes, what do you think you can do to stop translating?

   _____

   _____

5. Which of the six reading passages in units 4–6 did you
   enjoy most? Why?

   _____

   _____

6. Which of the six reading passages in units 4–6 was easiest?
   Which was most difficult? Why?

   _____

   _____

7. What improvements are you making as a reader? Look again at the
   "Tips for Fluent Reading" on pages 8 and 9. Write down one or
   two things that you know you can do better today than when you
   started this course.

   _____

   _____

8. What other improvements do you still want to make as a reader?

   _____

Review Reading 3: *Cell Phone and Internet Dangers*

Time yourself as you read through the passage. Try to read as fluently as you can. Record your time in the Reading Rate Chart on page 176. Then answer the questions on the following page.

http://www.asrinformation.heinle.com/dangers

Cell Phone and Internet Dangers

Cell phones and the Internet have improved our lives in many ways. However, along with improvements, they have also brought a number of worrying problems that need to be addressed.

5 Many car accidents are caused by cell phones. You can use many new cell phones to get on the Internet. This can be very convenient, but some drivers get on the Internet while driving. Driving needs all our attention. By looking at their cell phones and not at the road, these insensitive
10 drivers are a danger to us all.

Many of the dangers of the Internet are well known. Children who visit websites without their parents' permission sometimes talk to older people they don't know and put themselves in great danger. People with blogs sometimes post embarrassing photographs of people they do not know on their websites without permission. There are
15 also people who use the Internet to get personal information that we do not want them to have.

Cell Phone and Internet Safety Tips
▶ If you need to use a cell phone while you drive, use a "hands-free" phone.
▶ In difficult driving situations such as rain or snow, do not use your phone at all.
20 ▶ Do not make very important phone calls while driving. They take your attention off the road.
▶ Tell your children not to talk with anyone they do not know on the Internet.
▶ In an embarrassing situation, pay attention to people around you. People will be shy about taking your picture if they know you're paying attention.
▶ Refuse to give out any important personal information on the Internet.

270 words   Time taken _____

Reading Comprehension

1 The main point of this reading is
    a. to tell people why they shouldn't use cell phones or the Internet.
    b. to explain some technology concerns and ways to address them.
    c. to help people not to worry about using cell phones and the Internet.
    d. to show how technology has improved our lives.

2 Which of these dangers of cell phones or the Internet is not mentioned in the reading?
    a. You can have a car accident.
    b. Someone can post your photograph on the Internet.
    c. Someone can get your personal information.
    d. Someone you do not know can call you.

3 A "hands-free" cell phone is probably a cell phone that
    a. is free to use.
    b. can be used without your hands.
    c. can be used with only one hand.
    d. can be used only in cars.

4 While driving, it is safest to use your cell phone
    a. on a rainy day.
    b. to have a very important talk with your boss.
    c. in good weather with few cars around.
    d. to log on to the Internet.

5 Which of these pieces of advice on the Internet would the writer give to children?
    a. Don't talk with people you don't know.
    b. Visit websites only with your parents' permission.
    c. Don't give out your personal information.
    d. all of the above

6 What advice is given in the reading to stop someone from taking an embarrassing picture of you?
    a. Pay attention to the people around you.
    b. Don't give out your personal information.
    c. Use a "hands-free" cell phone.
    d. Wear your camera phone on your belt.

Fluency Practice

Time yourself as you read through the passage. Try to read as fluently as you can. Record your time in the Reading Rate Chart on page 176. Then answer the questions on the following page.

Selecting the Olympic Sports

There are 28 sports permitted in the Summer Olympic Games. The list of Olympic sports has many of the world's best-loved sports on it, such as baseball, judo, soccer, tennis, and volleyball.
5 This list of sports hadn't changed in 70 years, and the process for changing these sports is long and difficult.

That is why it was surprising news when the International Olympic Committee (IOC) announced that it was studying new sports for the list. At a meeting in Singapore in 2005,
10 the IOC voted on each of the 28 sports from the 2004 Olympic Games in Athens, Greece. Twenty-six of the 28 sports were selected for the 2012 Summer Olympic Games, which will take place in London, England. The two sports that did not receive 50 percent of the votes were baseball and softball.

Because these two sports were not selected, the IOC started the process of voting for two
15 new sports. The five sports to select from were roller skating, golf, rugby, squash, and karate. After the first vote, karate and squash were submitted to the IOC for the final vote.

To become an Olympic sport, a sport must receive two-thirds of the votes of the IOC. When the final vote took place, squash received 39 "yes" votes and 63 "no" votes. Karate received 38 "yes" votes and 63 "no" votes. This means that neither squash nor karate will feature in
20 the 2012 Olympic Games. This is sad, but fans of squash and karate still hope that their sports will be selected for the 2016 Olympic Games.

270 words   Time taken _____

Reading Comprehension

1 The main idea of this reading is how
   a. twenty-eight sports were selected for the 2012 Summer Olympic Games.
   b. two new sports were nearly selected for the 2012 Summer Olympic Games.
   c. two new sports were dropped from the Summer Olympic Games.
   d. five sports were selected as possible new Olympic sports.

2 At most, how many sports can there be in the Summer Olympic Games?
   a. 2
   b. 5
   c. 26
   d. 28

3 How many of the sports from the Athens Olympics were selected for the London Olympics?
   a. 2
   b. 5
   c. 26
   d. 39

4 Which of these statements is not true about baseball and softball?
   a. They were selected in 2005 for the London Olympics.
   b. They were part of the Athens Olympics.
   c. They didn't receive more than half of the IOC votes in Singapore.
   d. The IOC had to vote for new sports to take their place.

5 How many more votes did squash require in the last vote to become an Olympic sport?
   a. 28
   b. 29
   c. 63
   d. 102

6 Why was it surprising news when the IOC announced plans to change the list of Olympic sports?
   a. The list was very old and difficult to change.
   b. There are only 28 sports permitted in the Summer Olympic Games.
   c. Two sports did not receive 50 percent of the votes.
   d. The sports were the same as at the Athens Olympics.

Human Achievements

Hong Kong International Airport terminal is the largest in the world.

Singapore's Fountain of Wealth is the world's largest fountain.

The Galleria Vittorio Emanuele in Milan, Italy is probably the oldest shopping mall in the world.

Japan's Akashi-Kaikyo Bridge is the longest suspension bridge in the world.

Getting Ready

Discuss the following questions with a partner.

1 Have you ever seen any of the structures in the pictures above?
2 What other great human achievements like the places in the photos do you know? Which ones have you visited?
3 Where are the following things in your country: the oldest university; the tallest building; the largest museum; the largest library?
4 Are there any other great structures or buildings in your country?

Chapter 1: The World's Oldest University

Before You Read:

Al-Azhar University

A Discuss these questions with a partner before you look at the reading. Then write your guesses.

1 How old do you think the world's oldest university is?
_____

2 Where do you think it is?
_____

B Now scan the second paragraph of the reading and answer the following questions. Were your guesses correct?

1 What is the name of the world's oldest university?
_____

2 Where is the university?
_____

3 In what year was the university's first building built?
_____

4 In what year was the school started?
_____

5 Was Al-Azhar University started before or after A.D. 988?
_____

Reading Skill:

Recognizing Sequence of Events

In this passage, information is listed in the order that events happened. The sequence is shown with dates and a variety of words and phrases: "first," "in A.D. 972," "a few years later," "around the year 988," "in the years that followed," etc. These words make the order of events very clear for the reader.

A Without looking at the passage on the next page, put the events in the time line below in the correct order (1–7). Circle the words that helped you choose the correct order. Compare your answers with a partner.

University Time Line

	Then, leaders of the city thought of the idea for a school for higher learning.
	Scholars from around the world came to the university to study and do research.
	One of the first courses taught there was law.
1	The university was first built as a mosque in A.D. 972.
	The mosque was used as a meeting place for teachers.
	After that, Al-Azhar University was started.
	Today, the university is still important.

B Quickly skim the reading passage on the next page. Compare the events in the reading with the order of events in your time line above.

C Read the passage again and answer the questions that follow.

The World's Oldest University

Attending a university is an important part of a person's life. Today, many people go to a university to study and **train** for a future job in subjects[1] like law,[2] **medicine**, or education. But, the university is not a modern invention. An important one started in Egypt over one thousand years ago.

The world's oldest **surviving** university, Al-Azhar, is in Cairo, Egypt. It was 5 first built as a mosque[3] in A.D. 972 in honor of the daughter of the prophet Muhammad. A few years later, learners and teachers began meeting in the mosque in "tutoring circles." They read and talked about the subjects of religion and law. Around the year 988, leaders in the city of Cairo decided to create a school for higher learning and soon after that, Al-Azhar University was started. 10

Because a university was a new idea, the teachers at Al-Azhar needed to think about what courses[4] to teach and how to teach them. The earliest courses were in law and religion. In a course, students read and studied with the teacher, but there was also free discussion. Often, students and teachers had interesting discussions, and there was no "correct" answer. In the years that followed, the 15 new university **attracted** scholars[5] from around the world who came to teach and do **research**. At Al-Azhar, people studied the past, but it was also a place for sharing new ideas.

Over a thousand years later, Al-Azhar is still an important university in the world. Its library **contains** many of the world's oldest and most **valuable** books. 20 Today, many of the world's most important universities such as Oxford and Harvard still follow the same traditions as they do at Al-Azhar.

[1] **subject** something to study
[2] **law** the rules of a country
[3] **mosque** a building where followers of the Muslim religion go to pray
[4] **course** a group of lessons in a subject
[5] **scholar** a person who does studies at a high level

Reading Comprehension:
Check Your Understanding

A How much do you remember from the reading? Choose the best answer to complete each statement below.

1 The Al-Azhar mosque was built in honor of _____.
   a. the daughter of the prophet Muhammad
   b. teachers, learners, and scholars
   c. Cairo, Egypt
2 "Tutoring circles" are probably _____.
   a. groups of people who play music
   b. large spaces for students to use
   c. groups of teachers and students
3 The earliest courses at Al-Azhar were in _____.
   a. medicine and education
   b. law and religion
   c. Oxford and Harvard
4 Today, Al-Azhar University is _____.
   a. not a very important university
   b. only important because of its library
   c. still an important university in the world

B Decide if the following statements about the reading are true (*T*), false (*F*), or if the information is not given (*NG*). If you check (✓) false, correct the statement to make it true.

		T	F	NG
1	Today, many people go to a university to train for a future job.			
2	Tutoring circles included only teachers.			
3	At first, studying at Al-Azhar was expensive.			
4	Al-Azhar's library has many of the newest books.			

Critical Thinking

C Discuss these questions with your partner.
1 Before the first university was started, how did people teach and learn?
2 What kinds of books could you find in the Al-Azhar library?

Vocabulary Comprehension:
Odd Word Out

A For each group, circle the word that does not belong. The words in *italics* are vocabulary items from the reading.

1 be there   *attend*   take place
2 *attract*   select   choose
3 *contain*   spread   hold

4 concern	worry	*medicine*
5 study	*research*	vote
6 *survive*	live	work
7 experience	*training*	education
8 expensive	average	*valuable*

B Answer these questions. Share your ideas with a partner.

1 What are some other things you can *attend*? _____
2 Besides books, what does a library *contain*? _____
3 What kind of *training* would you like to have? _____
4 Name some popular *medicines*. _____

A Complete the chart with the missing parts of speech. Use your dictionary to help you. Compare your answers with a partner.

	Noun	Verb	Adjective
1	_____	attract	_____
2	attendance	_____	_____
3	_____	worry	_____
4	embarrassment	_____	_____
5	_____	_____	permissible
6	_____	_____	exciting

Vocabulary Skill:
Word Families

When you learn a new word in English, it is helpful to learn words in the same "family" that form different parts of speech. Learning all these parts of speech can help you to build your vocabulary.

B Now choose the correct word from the chart to complete the following sentences. Be sure to use the correct form of each word.

1 I'm really _____ about my father. He's been sick for three weeks.
2 You cannot hunt animals in this country unless you have a hunting _____.
3 Marlo's sister is very _____. She looks like a movie star!
4 Students planning to _____ classes must first pay the $50 fee.
5 My brother took a wrong turn and went into the women's bathroom. He was so _____.
6 I'm going to study abroad next year. I'm really _____ about it. It's awesome!

Before You Read:
Great Engineering

A Answer the following questions.

1 Look at these five wonders of modern engineering. What do you think they are?

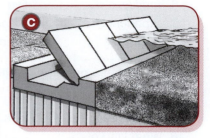

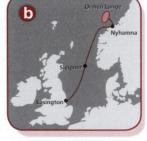

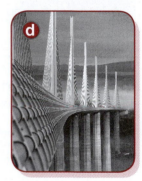

2 Scan the reading on page 93 and find the five subtitles. Match the subtitles with the pictures above.

B Discuss your answers with a partner.

Reading Skill:
Scanning

When we scan we move our eyes over a text and only stop and read the parts that we are looking for. We could scan a newspaper or a television guide, for example, or we could scan to find information for a test. Readings or web pages with subtitled sections can be easier to scan.

A What is the location of the following engineering wonders? Scan the reading for the locations and write them in the chart.

Engineering wonder	Location	Year of Completion
1 Falkirk Wheel		
2 Millau Viaduct		
3 Langeled Pipeline		
4 Three Gorges Dam		
5 Venice Tide Barrier		

B Next scan the reading again to find the years of completion for these engineering wonders and write them in the chart.

C Read the passage again and answer the questions that follow.

http://www.ACTIVEwonders.heinle.com

21st Century Wonders of Engineering

Great Engineering has selected five wonders[1] of 21st century engineering for our Excellence Prize. Now we're asking you to vote for one and tell us why!

Falkirk Wheel (Falkirk, Scotland 2001)

The Falkirk **Wheel** is the world's only **rotating** boat lift. Its steel arms each hold a water-filled tank into which boats can sail.[2] As the wheel rotates, so do the arms, raising and lowering the boats a distance of 25 meters, using power equal to only eight **boiling** tea kettles.[3]

Millau Viaduct (Millau, France 2005)

The 2.46-kilometer-long Millau Viaduct over the River Tam in the south of France is 270 meters high—perhaps the highest bridge in the world. It was built in just three years. It is a beautiful bridge that adds to the natural beauty of the river valley.

Langeled Pipeline (The North Sea 2007)

This pipeline[4] under the ocean carries natural gas across the 1,200 kilometers of rocky sea bed from Norway to Britain. It is the longest pipeline of its kind. It runs through some of the most dangerous waters in the world.

Three Gorges Dam (Yichang, China 2009)

Three Gorges Dam is the largest dam for electric power in the world. Its 1.6-kilometer-long wall across the Yangtze River rises 183 meters above the valley floor. It can hold back 39 million cubic meters of water.

Venice Tide Barrier (Venice, Italy 2011)

In 1966, the city of Venice was **flooded** in two meters of ocean water. To prevent this happening again, the Italian government is planning to build 78 walls, each about 600 square meters, that will rise from the sea floor when the water level of the Adriatic Sea is dangerously high and **threatens** the city.

[1]**wonder** something very special and amazing

[2]**sail** move as a ship or boat moves

[3]**tea kettle** a pot used to make hot water for tea or other hot drinks

[4]**pipeline** a long pipe that carries oil, gas, etc. a long distance

Reading Comprehension:
Check Your Understanding

A How much do you remember from the reading? Match each fact with the engineering wonder it describes.

1 It is the longest one in the world. _____   **a.** Falkirk Wheel
2 It creates electric power. _____   **b.** Millau Viaduct
3 It has 78 walls. _____   **c.** Langeled Pipeline
4 It uses surprisingly little power. _____   **d.** Three Gorges Dam
5 It was built in three years. _____   **e.** Venice Tide Barrier

B Complete the sentences with information from the reading. Write no more than three words for each answer.

1 The Tide Barrier is necessary because in 1966 the city of Venice was

_____.

2 The Falkirk Wheel is a rotating _____.
3 The Langeled Pipeline carries natural gas from _____ to _____.

Critical Thinking

C Discuss these questions with your partner.

1 What are some examples of excellent engineering in your city or town? Why do you think they are excellent?
2 Explain why it was necessary to plan and build each of these engineering wonders. Why were they or are they needed?

Vocabulary Comprehension:
Words in Context

A The words in *italics* are vocabulary items from the reading. Read each question or statement and choose the correct answer. Check your answers with a partner.

1 I first need to *boil* the water when I want to _____.
   a. make some tea   **b.** take a shower
2 A *century* is _____.
   a. 100 years   **b.** 1,000 years
3 *Engineers* can _____.
   a. build bridges   **b.** make clothes
4 During a *flood* there is a lot of _____ in the streets.
   a. water   **b.** noise
5 A *prize* is usually given _____.
   a. to winners of a competition   **b.** to all engineering students
6 A *rotating* sign goes _____.
   a. around and around   **b.** up and down
7 The man was *threatening* to _____.
   a. hit me   **b.** give me a present
8 Typically, there aren't any *wheels* on a _____.
   a. bicycle   **b.** sled

B Complete the sentences using the words in *italics* from A. Be sure to use the correct form of the word.

1 A minute after the car accident, the _____ on the car were still _____.

2 The power of the water was so strong that nobody survived the _____.

3 The United States has been a country for more than two _____.

4 Three men _____ to kill me if I didn't give them my money.

A There are a few rules to follow when forming superlatives. Look at the examples below.

1 When an adjective has *one syllable* the superlative is formed by adding *-est*.

| tall → the tallest | neat → the neatest |

2 When an adjective *ends* in -e, form the superlative by adding *-st*.

| nice → the nicest | large → the largest |

3 When a one-syllable adjective ends in a consonant-vowel-consonant pattern, we double the last consonant and add *-est*.

| big → the biggest | thin → the thinnest |

4 When an adjective has two syllables and ends in *-y*, the superlative is formed by changing the *-y* to *i* and adding *-est*.

| pretty → the prettiest | easy → the easiest |

5 When an adjective has two or more syllables and does not end in *-y*, put "*the most*" before it.

| curious → the most curious | expensive → the most expensive |

6 Other common adjectives have irregular superlative forms.

| good → the best | bad → the worst | far → the farthest |

B Look at the adjectives below. Write the number of the rule you would follow to form the superlative next to each word.

_____ delicious	_____ useful	_____ valuable	_____ convenient
_____ funny	_____ cool	_____ long	_____ hot
_____ large	_____ angry	_____ shy	_____ high
_____ messy	_____ simple	_____ bad	_____ sad
_____ important	_____ excellent	_____ rude	_____ far

C Now use the adjectives in B or ones of your own to write sentences with superlatives like the ones below. Then read them to a partner.

1 I think **Italian food** is **the most delicious** of all.

2 **Jim Carrey** is **the funniest man** that I know.

Vocabulary Skill:
Superlative Adjectives

When we want to compare one thing or person to all the others in a group, we use the superlative form of an adjective. For example, "the tallest building in the world," "the youngest person in this class." Superlatives can be formed in different ways. All superlatives have "the" in front of them.

Real Life Skill:
Recognizing Survey
Question Types

Many organizations make surveys to collect information about people's views and opinions. These polls or surveys are organized in different ways. Knowing some of the different types of surveys used can help you to understand them better.

A Look at the different ways of asking for information about spare time activities. Match each question to its type below.

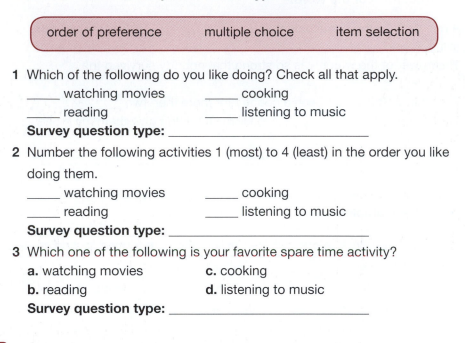

order of preference   multiple choice   item selection

1 Which of the following do you like doing? Check all that apply.
_____ watching movies   _____ cooking
_____ reading   _____ listening to music
Survey question type: _____

2 Number the following activities 1 (most) to 4 (least) in the order you like doing them.
_____ watching movies   _____ cooking
_____ reading   _____ listening to music
Survey question type: _____

3 Which one of the following is your favorite spare time activity?
a. watching movies   **c.** cooking
b. reading   **d.** listening to music
Survey question type: _____

B Work in a small group. Together, rank the wonders on page 93 from 1 (most wonderful) to 5 (least wonderful). Then compare your ranking with another group.

C Internet Challenge: Look for examples of survey question types online. Find examples of different online survey question types. Take notes on the types of questions you find. If possible, print out examples. Present the information you find to the class. For your Internet search words, use *sample survey* or your own idea.

What Do You Think?

1 We have talked about human achievements in the areas of education and engineering. What are some examples of great human achievements in art, music, and literature?
2 What kinds of achievements do you think will be made in medicine and health?
3 Can you imagine any further achievements in public transportation or space travel?
4 What kinds of achievements do you think are the most important for humans to work on in the 21st century?

ZDRAVSTVUITE!

Bom dia! *Aloha!*

Ni hao! Bonjour!

Konnichiwa!

Guten tag! Annyong ha shimnikka!

Hola! Namaste!

Getting Ready

Discuss the following questions with a partner.

1 Look at the ways to say "Hello!" in ten languages above. Which ones do you know? Which languages are they from?
2 How many other ways of saying "Hello!" do you know?
3 How many languages can you speak? Which others do you wish you could speak?
4 What are the most popular languages to study in your country?

Unit 8

Chapter 1: Which English Will We Speak?

Before You Read:
Languages without Borders

A Match each group of countries with the language they share.

1 Austria, Germany, Liechtenstein _____   a. Portuguese
2 Egypt, Syria, Yemen _____   b. Spanish
3 Chile, Colombia, Cuba _____   c. Arabic
4 Brazil, Cape Verde, Portugal _____   d. English
5 Australia, Barbados, Jamaica _____   e. German

B Answer the following questions with a partner.

1 In which countries around the world is English a first language? Make a list.
2 Do you know of any differences between the English spoken in these countries? Give some examples.
3 The passage on the next page talks about three different groups of countries that use English in different ways. Scan the reading to find the countries and write them in the chart.

Group 1	Group 2	Group 3

Reading Skill:
Identifying Main Ideas

When we read, we try to make connections between what we are reading and what we already know. It is easier to make those connections if we know the main idea of what we are reading about.

A Look at this list of key words that are repeated in the article on the next page. Scan the article on the next page to find them. How many times can you find each one?

1 language _____   3 speakers _____
2 English _____   4 countries _____

B Skim the article quickly. Read only the *title*, the *first paragraph*, the *first sentence of the middle paragraphs*, and the *last paragraph*. Don't worry about words you don't know. Then complete the sentence below.

The main idea of this reading is _____.
a. The most important type of English continues to be British English.
b. There are many types of English, and they will continue to change.
c. English will not be the international language for too much longer.

C Now read the passage, then answer the questions that follow.

Which English Will We Speak?

Although English is called the "international language," there are actually quite a few **varieties** of English that exist around the world. English, of course, **originated** in England; but soon English spread to all of Britain, and different varieties began to exist. Varieties of English that are often taught to language students are British, American, Canadian, Irish, Australian, and New Zealand. 5
Native speakers of English from these countries number more than 380 million.

There is a second group of countries that have their own varieties of English. Their histories have been directly touched by one of the English-speaking **civilizations**. Therefore, they use English in various important ways within their own government and everyday life. India, Malaysia, the Philippines, and Kenya 10
are examples of this group. The total number of speakers in this group is more than 300 million.

In a third group of countries, English is widely used as a foreign language. However, citizens use their native language within their own government and in everyday life. Some countries in this group are China, Russia, Japan, Korea, 15
Egypt, Indonesia, and the countries of Western Europe. Some people **calculate** the number of speakers in this group to be as many as one billion—and it is growing fast.

This changing **situation** of English raises many questions. Will people continue to **admire** the English of countries such as Britain or the United States? Will 20
another language **replace** English as the international language? Will new varieties of English **develop** in other countries such as China or Russia? Or, in future centuries, will a new international variety of English develop that doesn't belong to any one country—one that is spoken just as correctly in Asia or Africa as in Europe? 25

Reading Comprehension:
Check Your Understanding

A **The statements below are about the reading. Choose the correct answer to complete each one.**

1 Britain, America, Canada, Ireland, Australia, and New Zealand are countries _____.
   a. where the number of English-speakers is growing
   b. whose English is often taught to language learners
   c. that continue to admire the English of Britain

2 Countries whose histories have been directly touched by one of the English-speaking civilizations use English _____.
   a. in government only
   b. in everyday life only
   c. in both government and everyday life

3 In China and Russia, English is widely used _____.
   a. in everyday life
   b. in government and everyday life
   c. as a foreign language

4 The writer of the passage asks if _____.
   a. English will continue to be the international language
   b. new languages will develop in Asia, Africa, and Europe
   c. Russian will become the new international language

B **Decide if the following statements about the reading are true (*T*), false (*F*), or if the information is not given (*NG*). If you check (✓) false, correct the statement to make it true.**

	T	F	NG
1 The world needs another international language.			
2 The Philippines have their own variety of English.			
3 English is widely used as a foreign language in Egypt.			
4 English is the main language of the government of Indonesia.			

Critical Thinking

C **Discuss these questions with your partner.**

1 Do you think it is important for the world to have an international language? Why or why not?

2 Do you think another language will replace English as the international language in the future? Explain your reasons.

A Look at the list of words and phrases from the reading. Match each one with a definition on the right.

1 admire _____   a. to work with numbers
2 calculate _____   b. to grow or change over time
3 civilization _____   c. to take the place of
4 develop _____   d. how things are
5 originate _____   e. to like very much
6 replace _____   f. to start
7 situation _____   g. type or sort
8 variety _____   h. a country or large group of people with their own customs and ways of living

B Now complete the sentences below using the words from A. Be sure to use the correct form of the word.

1 Many people _____ the great art and buildings of the European _____.
2 The workers took out the blue flowers and _____ them with a red _____.
3 The flood created a very dangerous _____ for people and animals.
4 This river _____ high in the mountains.

A Look at these English words from other languages. Practice saying them with a partner. Can you add any more to the chart?

Language	Loan word	Language	Loan word
French	passport	Dutch	cruise
Turkish	kiosk	Korean	kimchi
Latin	candle	Japanese	tsunami
Italian	violin	Malay	ketchup
Spanish	mosquito	Chinese	tea
German	hamburger	Inuit	kayak

There are many words in English that have come from other languages. These are called loan words and they are now used as part of everyday English.

B Complete the sentences below using the words from A. Use your dictionary to help you if you do not know the exact meaning of the words. Be sure to use the correct form of the word.

1 Please boil some water. I would like to have some _____.
2 A _____ is a very small animal that drinks blood.
3 _____ is made from vegetables; there are many varieties.
4 I would like some _____ on my _____.
5 Please show me your _____ before you board the plane.
6 I bought a magazine at the _____.
7 The city was flooded by the _____.
8 My favorite music in the world is _____ music.

Chapter 2: Sign Language

A Look at this sign language alphabet. Practice making these signs with your hand.

B Use the sign language to spell English words to a partner.

Reading Skill:

Distinguishing Main Idea and Supporting Details

Many paragraphs have a main idea that is supported by a number of details. Not all details in a paragraph support the main idea; some support the supporting ideas themselves. Finding the main and supporting ideas helps us clearly understand the writer's point.

A Look at the main idea and one supporting detail from the first paragraph of the article on the next page. Write the two missing supporting details.

Main idea: Deaf people have special ways of communicating

Supporting details:

1 _____

2 speaking with voice training

3 _____

B Now write the main idea and five supporting details for the second paragraph.

Main idea: _____

1 _____
2 _____
3 _____
4 _____
5 _____

C Read the passage and answer the questions that follow.

Sign Language

Because deaf people cannot hear, they have special ways of **communicating**. One way is lip reading. With training, people can learn to understand what someone is saying by looking at the mouth of the speaker. Speaking is possible but difficult for the deaf. Because they cannot hear their own voices, it takes a lot of training to be able to make the correct sounds, and not all deaf people can **get the hang** 5 **of** this skill. But, the way of communicating that deaf people all around the world seem to think is the most **practical** is sign language.

In many ways, sign language is **similar** to spoken languages. The "words" of sign language are its signs. The signs are formed with movements of the hands, face, and body. As with words, each sign has a different meaning. Signs are combined 10 to form sentences. The alphabet of sign language is hand signs that **stand for** letters; they make spelling possible. The signs combine to form a rich language that can express the same thoughts, feelings, and **intentions** as a spoken language. And just as different countries usually speak different languages, most countries have their own **variation** of sign language. 15

In addition to knowing sign language, it is also helpful to know something about how deaf people communicate. Hand waving or hitting a table or the floor to get someone's attention is fine. Also, lots of eye contact[1] is necessary. Hellos and goodbyes for deaf people are not **formal**; they are long and full of touching and joking. Lastly, it is good to remember that most deaf people do not think of 20 themselves as different from other people, and you don't have to either!

[1]**eye contact** looking into another person's eyes

Reading Comprehension:

Check Your Understanding

A How much do you remember from the reading? Complete the following statements using the correct words and phrases.

1 For deaf people, _____ is possible but difficult.
2 Most countries have their own _____ of sign language.
3 If a deaf man wants to get your attention, he might _____ a table.
4 Deaf people aren't _____ from other people.

B Decide if the following statements about the reading are true (*T*) or false (*F*). If you check (✓) false, correct the statement to make it true.

		T	F
1	Only deaf people can learn how to lip read.		
2	Lots of eye contact is necessary for deaf people.		
3	Signs are combined to form letters.		
4	Signs are formed by movements of the hands, face, and body.		

Critical Thinking

C Discuss these questions with your partner.
1 Think of all the things you do in an average day. Which ones couldn't you do if you were deaf?
2 How can deaf people manage to survive without hearing alarm clocks, doorbells, and telephones?

Vocabulary Comprehension:

Words in Context

A The words in *italics* are vocabulary items from the reading. Read each question or statement and choose the best answer. Compare your answers with a partner.

1 If you *get the hang* of something, you learn to do it _____.
   a. well   **b.** poorly
2 *Practical* advice is useful _____.
   a. mostly in books   **b.** in everyday life
3 My sister and I are very *similar*; we like mostly _____ things.
   a. the same   **b.** different
4 What do _____ *stand for*?
   a. the numbers 123   **b.** the letters ATM
5 *Variation* is important in school lunches; the students need _____ each day.
   a. different foods   **b.** the same foods
6 If it is your *intention* to have dinner, then you _____.
   a. are planning to eat   **b.** might eat if you're hungry
7 When you *communicate*, you _____ ideas.
   a. admire   **b.** share
8 _____ is an example of *formal* clothes.
   a. a baseball cap   **b.** a necktie

B Answer these questions. Share your answers with a partner.

1 What are some other examples of formal clothes? _____
2 How are you similar to people in your family? _____
3 What letters do you know that stand for something? _____
4 What are some ways that animals communicate? _____

A Complete the chart with the missing parts of speech. Use your dictionary to help you. Compare your answers with a partner.

Noun	Verb	Adjective
1. intention	_____	_____
2. _____	_____	practical
3. _____	threaten	_____
4. _____	imagine	_____
5. harm	_____	_____
6. _____	_____	communicative

Vocabulary Skill:
Word Families

When you learn a new word in English, it is helpful to also learn words that are related to it. Learning the different parts of speech that form the word family can help you expand your vocabulary.

B Now choose the correct word from the chart to complete the following sentences. Be sure to use the correct form of each word.

1 _____ is the key to a happy marriage.
2 Smoking can cause serious _____ to your health.
3 You'll never get the hang of playing the violin if you don't _____.
4 Please don't be angry at me for taking a wrong turn. It wasn't _____.
5 Some 21st century engineers must have a lot of _____ to create such wonderful and amazing things.
6 The thief _____ to hurt me if I didn't give him my money.

Real Life Skill:
Reading Signs and Symbols

One very common way of communicating without words is by using symbols. Many signs in public places use symbols so you can understand them even if you can't speak the language. Some of these signs are the same around the world, but others are only used in one country.

A Here are some signs commonly seen in English-speaking countries. Write the meaning under each one.

school area	restaurant	airport
hotel	for disabled people	no parking
no smoking	danger—electricity	information
restrooms	crossing	no drinking

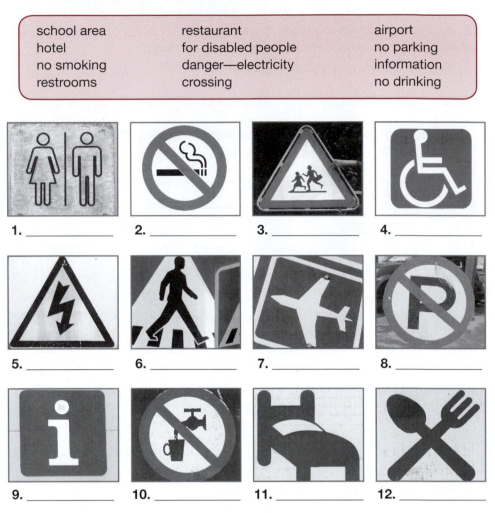

1. _____   2. _____   3. _____   4. _____

5. _____   6. _____   7. _____   8. _____

9. _____   10. _____   11. _____   12. _____

B Talk to a partner. Where would you see each of these signs?

C Which of these symbols are used in your country? Write the numbers.

What Do You Think?

1 Do you use a lot of gestures when you speak? Which ones do you use?
2 Is there anything about the sounds and gestures typical of English speakers that you find difficult to do yourself?
3 Does English make a good or a bad international language? What are its good points and bad points as an international language?

Festivals and Celebrations

Spring—Spring Festival, China

Summer—Los Sanfermines, Spain

Winter—Mardi Gras, Brazil

Fall—Thanksgiving Day, the United States

Getting Ready

Discuss the following questions with a partner.

1 Which of the festivals above do you know about? What do you know about them?
2 What is happening in each of the pictures?
3 Name another famous festival or celebration for spring, summer, fall, and winter.
4 What is your favorite festival? Why do you like it?

Chapter 1: How Do You Celebrate?

Before You Read:
Time to Party!

A Read the statements below. Do you think they are true (*T*) or false (*F*)? Check (✓) the correct box.

		T	F
1	People in many Western countries make promises to change their lives in the New Year.		
2	In some countries a festival called Carnival is celebrated in January or February.		
3	Carnival first started in Brazil.		
4	At Carnival people wear costumes and dance.		
5	The two biggest Carnivals are now held in Brazil and the United States.		

B Compare your answers with a partner.

Reading Skill:
Scanning

When we scan we look for information that we want and ignore other information. This saves time. On tests, scanning can be useful when checking if a fact is true or false, or to find the place in a reading about which a question is asked.

A Scan the reading passage on the next page to find out if the statements in Before You Read above are really true or false. Share your answers with a partner.

B Scan the reading to find and complete these expressions from the reading.

1 _____ goodbye
   a. tell   **b.** share   **c.** say
2 _____ promises
   a. have   **b.** make   **c.** teach
3 _____ time
   a. use   **b.** lose   **c.** spend
4 _____ night
   a. all   **b.** whole   **c.** total
5 _____ place
   a. get   **b.** take   **c.** receive
6 _____ the party
   a. enter   **b.** jump   **c.** join

C Read the passage again, then answer the questions that follow.

How Do You Celebrate?

Mardi Gras celebration

People everywhere celebrate the New Year. Although there are variations in the way they **celebrate**, for most it is a time to say goodbye to the past and to think about new beginnings. In many countries, people get together with family and friends on December 31 to eat, drink, dance, **socialize**, and welcome January 1 at midnight. 5

In many Western countries people make New Year's resolutions. They make promises to themselves to make changes in their lives over the coming year, such as to lose weight, to stop smoking, to get a new job, or to learn a new skill. In many Asian countries, people also celebrate the New Year in late January or early February. People spend time with family and eat special foods. In most 10 countries, the holiday lasts for several days.

In late February or early March, some countries celebrate a special **festival** called Carnival. Many think that Carnival first started in Italy or Greece. People dressed in costumes, wore colorful **masks**, ate, drank, and danced all night on the Tuesday before the start of Lent, 40 days of **sacrifice** of **pleasure** 15 before Easter. This tradition spread to France, Spain, Portugal, and later, to Brazil and the United States.

Now, two of the biggest Carnivals take place in Rio de Janeiro in Brazil, and New Orleans in the United States. People still wear **flashy** costumes, and at Carnival in Rio there is a very long **parade** that lasts for four days. 20

In New Orleans, Carnival is called Mardi Gras, which translates to "fat Tuesday" and lasts for three weeks. Both celebrations combine music and traditions from all over the world. Millions of visitors travel from around the world to join the party.

Reading Comprehension:

Check Your Understanding

A The statements below are about the reading. Complete each one using the correct word or phrase.

1 A New Year's resolution is a _____ to yourself to change your life.
2 A typical New Year's resolution might be to lose _____.
3 In many Asian countries, the New Year's holiday lasts for _____.
4 The first Carnival possibly took place in _____.

B Are the following statements about New Year or Carnival celebrations? Check (✓) *NY* or *C*.

	NY	C
1 Some people try to stop smoking.		
2 It is a Western tradition.		
3 In one city it lasts for three weeks.		
4 People spend time with family.		

Critical Thinking

C Discuss these questions with your partner.
1 What are some other good ideas for New Year's resolutions?
2 Why do you think the Mardi Gras became most popular in New Orleans but not in other cities in the United States?

Vocabulary Comprehension:

Word Definitions

A Match a word from the reading with a definition. Write the letter of the definition next to the word.

1 socialize _____
2 pleasure _____
3 mask _____
4 festival _____
5 sacrifice _____
6 parade _____
7 celebrate _____
8 flashy _____

a. to not have or not do something you like, usually for your own good or the good of others
b. very bright and colorful
c. to mix with other people
d. to have a party for a happy reason
e. this covers your face or eyes at a party
f. a very big, traditional party
g. something that feels good or is fun
h. people walking down the street together with music and costumes

B Complete each sentence below using one of the words from A. Be sure to use the correct form of the word.

1 Western civilization _____ the New Year on January 1.

2 Carnival is a _____ that is celebrated every year in Rio de Janeiro.

3 Mark is smiling because it's a great _____ for him to spend the day with his family.

4 I admire people who _____ their free time to help older people.

A Look at how different prepositions are used with different time expressions.

> **In**
>
> Use *in* with months, seasons, years, some parts of the day, and periods of time in the future, for example: *in December, in spring, in the morning,* * *in 1975, in four months.* *except at night

> **On**
>
> Use *on* with days of the week, specific dates, special days, and other time expressions, for example: *on Monday*, *on December 15*, *on Christmas Day*, *on the weekend*.

> **At**
>
> Use *at* with exact times of day and in expressions like *at work*, *at home*, and *at school*.

B Complete the sentences below using the correct prepositions.

1 Guess what happened _____ Friday! I won first prize in the beauty contest!

2 I have to take my medicine _____ exactly 7:00. Don't let me forget!

3 We need to submit that report _____ February 12.

4 My interview process begins _____ two weeks.

5 I can't attend that concert because I'm going to be _____ work.

6 I had a really bad car accident _____ October.

7 I paid a lot of taxes _____ 2006.

C Now complete these sentences about yourself using the correct time preposition and a time expression.

1 My birthday is _____ _____.

2 I usually go on vacation _____ _____.

3 I usually eat breakfast _____ _____.

4 I typically go to bed _____ _____.

5 _____ New Year's Day I always _____.

6 My mother was born _____ _____ and my father was born _____ _____.

Vocabulary Skill:
Prepositions of Time: *in, on, at*

When we talk about the time that we do things, we usually use prepositions. The most common prepositions are "in," "on," and "at." Learning the basic rules of how they are used will help you to get them right.

Chapter 2: My Songkran Festival Journal

Before You Read:
An Interesting Culture

A What country did the writer of the journal on the next page visit? Scan the journal for key words that can let you know the country.

B Discuss the following questions with a partner.

1 Look at the photo of the *wai*. What does this gesture mean?
2 Look at the photo of a *wat*. What is this building used for?

The *wai*

A *wat*

Reading Skill:
Reading for Details

When reading for details, we read every word and make sure to understand the meaning. Reading for details is especially useful when we need to get information from one part of a larger reading. We can scan the reading for the part we need to read for details. We often need to do this when taking tests.

A Scan the journal on the next page. Check (✓) three things that happened on April 12.

1 ☐ Paul had some delicious food.
2 ☐ Worawut translated for Paul.
3 ☐ Paul stayed in a hotel.
4 ☐ Worawut's family did spring cleaning.
5 ☐ They all built a wooden house.
6 ☐ The family greeted Paul.

B Check (✓) three things they did on April 14.

1 ☐ They filled the bowls of some monks.
2 ☐ They attended a music concert.
3 ☐ They sacrificed their breakfast.
4 ☐ They poured water over stone Buddhas.
5 ☐ They used sand to make sand pagodas.
6 ☐ They took a bath.

C Now read the entire passage and answer the questions that follow.

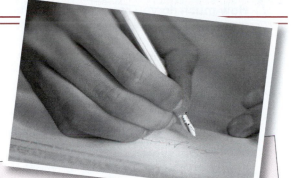

Paul's Songkran Festival Journal

April 12

Today I arrived at my friend Worawut's house outside of Bangkok for the holidays.
His family was doing a spring cleaning of their pretty wooden house in preparation
for the spring festival of Songkran. They put their hands together to **greet** me with
a traditional gesture called the wai. Worawut translated their words for me.   5

April 13

That smells wonderful! The women were cooking Thai foods for the next day's
ceremonies. We men went to the river and brought lots of **sand** to the village wat.
The wat was a beautiful Buddhist building where the monks[1] lived. We left the sand in
piles near the wat. Worawut said I'd soon find out why.   10

April 14

We all dressed up and went to the village wat. The monks waited with their bowls
at a long table. Monks are used to a life of sacrifice and **discipline**, but not today.
We filled their bowls with rice and all kinds of delicious foods. Everyone smiled and
music played as the monks ate.   15
After that, we attended the **bathing** ceremony. We **poured** water over little stone
Buddhas. Young people poured some sweet smelling water into the hands of older
people to show respect for them.
Outside, everyone used the sand we had brought to make sand pagodas.[2] We put   20
flowers, **flags**, and stones on ours. It was beautiful!

April 15

Today was the last day of the festival, and Worawut told me to get ready for some
water throwing. We put lots of buckets of water on the truck and drove into the
village. Everyone was throwing buckets of water. Nobody escaped dry! On such a   25
hot day, the water felt really good. I can't wait to come back next year!

[1] **monk** a man who lives in a religious community away from the rest of society
[2] **pagoda** a tall religious building (usually Buddhist)

Reading Comprehension:
Check Your Understanding

A How much do you remember from the reading? Choose the best answer for each question or statement below.

1 Worawut is Paul's _____.
   a. friend   **b.** student   **c.** boss
2 Paul probably _____ Thai food.
   a. usually eats   **b.** doesn't like   **c.** likes
3 In line 13, "We filled their bowls with rice and all kinds of delicious foods," "their" means _____.
   a. everybody's   **b.** the monks'   **c.** Worawut's family's
4 The throwing of water made Paul feel _____.
   a. embarrassed   **b.** happy   **c.** angry

B Number these events 1 to 4 in the order they happened.

_____ They went to throw water in the village.
_____ The men brought sand to the *wat*.
_____ They attended the bathing ceremony.
_____ Everybody made sand pagodas.

Critical Thinking

C Discuss these questions with your partner.
1 In Thailand, how do the people probably feel about the monks?
2 What do you think about a festival in which everybody throws water at everybody? Would you like to participate?

Vocabulary Comprehension:
Odd Word Out

A For each group, circle the word that does not belong. The words in *italics* are vocabulary items from the reading.

1 *bathe*	swim	work
2 preparation	*discipline*	strictness
3 *greet*	welcome	express
4 shirt	*flag*	pants
5 valley	hill	*pile*
6 *pour*	rotate	flood
7 wheel	*sand*	dirt
8 *ceremony*	celebration	education

B Complete the sentences using the words in *italics* from A. Be sure to use the correct form of the word.

1 You need to have _____ to sacrifice pleasure.
2 On top of every government building you can see our country's _____.
3 Waitress! Could you please _____ me another cup of coffee?
4 I _____ my dog every month. If I don't, he has a terrible smell.

A Look at the pictures below and write the correct sense under each one.

Vocabulary Skill:

Sensory Verbs

The five senses are sight, sound, smell, taste, and touch. There are many verbs in English associated with these senses. They often have differences in meaning and are used in different ways. For example, you "watch TV" but "look at" a painting.

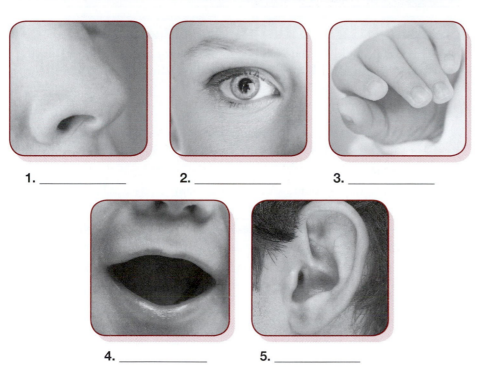

1. _____

2. _____

3. _____

4. _____

5. _____

B Now match the verbs below to the senses. Write the number of the picture next to each verb.

listen	hear	lick	look	feel	touch
watch	smell	taste	see	sniff	

C Complete the sentences below with the correct verb from B above. Be sure to use the correct form of the verb.

1 There's a good movie on TV tonight. Do you want to _____ it?

2 We're going to _____ a Picasso exhibition at the museum tomorrow.

3 This medicine _____ terrible.

4 Is someone _____ to the radio? I can _____ music.

5 A little baby's skin always _____ so soft when you _____ it.

Real Life Skill:
Reading Tourist Information

Many cities have a Visitors' Bureau or Tourist Information Center. They have brochures and websites about places to visit, sightseeing tours, festivals, and events. Understanding some of the language commonly used in the information can help you plan your trip better.

A Read this brochure about a festival.

CELEBRATE MARDI GRAS IN NEW ORLEANS!

Mardi Gras is held on the Tuesday 46 days before Easter. The 12 days before it are filled with over 70 parades of dazzling floats—there are 9 parades on the day of Mardi Gras alone!

<u>Tips</u> for visitors:

- Plan ahead: Many hotels start taking reservations for Mardi Gras in August. To get the room you want, call <u>well in advance</u>. Don't wait until January!

- Plan your transportation: Remember that many streets are closed to cars.

- Get there early: For the big parades on the weekend before Mardi Gras, plan to arrive about four hours ahead of time. For the Sunday Night Parade at 6 P.M., you will need to find a good <u>spot</u> in the morning.

- Check the weather forecasts: It can be very warm or very cold at this time of year. You might need a jacket, <u>sunscreen</u>, or an umbrella—or all three.

- Catch Mardi Gras "throws": People riding on floats in the parades give "throws" to the crowd. <u>Spectators</u> jump up to catch beads, plastic coins, cups, and toy animals. Bring a plastic bag to hold all your treasures.

B Match each underlined word in the brochure with its meaning below.

1 cream or lotion that protects your skin from the sun _____
2 pieces of useful information _____
3 space; place _____
4 a long time before _____
5 people who watch an event _____

C Circle true (*T*) or false (*F*). Then circle the information in the brochure that helped you find the answer.

1 The weather is always good in New Orleans at this time of year.   T   F
2 You should make hotel reservations for Mardi Gras in January.   T   F
3 You can get lots of free souvenirs at the parades.   T   F
4 All of the parades are held on one day.   T   F

What Do You Think?

1 What do you usually do on national holidays?
2 Do you think there are enough national holidays?
3 Were festivals more important in the past than they are now?
4 How has modern technology changed festivals?

Fluency Strategy: *Dealing with Unknown Words*

If you stop to learn every new word you read, you will slow down your reading fluency. It is often possible to skip unknown words when you read.

A Read the first paragraph of the article "Amazing Machines" and underline any words you do not know the meanings of. As you underline the words, keep reading with your eyes moving fluently over the text.

The Deepest Diving Submarine

The Japanese research submarine Shinkai 6500 can dive deeper than any other submarine. On August 11, 1989, it plunged to a depth of 6,526 meters beneath the ocean's surface. Three occupants can ride in the submarine, which is 9.5 meters long, 2.7 meters wide, and 3.2 meters high. It is used for ocean research all over the world.

5

B Look at the words that you underlined in the paragraph above and complete the chart below.

Unknown word	Line number	Unknown word	Line number

Did you underline any word more than once? If a new word comes up several times while reading, then it may be important to pause and think about its meaning. For example, the word "submarine" appears four times. Did you already know what it means? If not, can you guess its meaning from the paragraph?

C Now answer this comprehension question about the paragraph you just read:

1 What is **not** true about the submarine Shinkai 6500?
   a. It is used only in Japan.
   b. It can dive deeper than other submarines.
   c. Three people can ride in it.
   d. It is 9.5 meters long.

Were you able to answer this question without looking up the meaning of the unknown word(s)? Remember, you don't always need to understand every word to understand the meaning of the passage.

D Now read the whole article on the next page, without using a dictionary. Underline any words you don't know, but don't worry about their meaning. How many words did you skip? _____ Write the words you underlined here. _____

Amazing Machines

The Deepest Diving Submarine

The Japanese research submarine Shinkai 6500 can dive deeper than any other submarine. On August 11, 1989, it plunged to a depth of 6,526

5 meters beneath the ocean's surface. Three occupants can ride in the submarine, which is 9.5 meters long, 2.7 meters wide, and 3.2 meters high. It is used for ocean research all over the world.

The World's Most Intelligent Vacuum Cleaner

10 The Dyson DC06 vacuum cleaner can clean your floor by itself and save you valuable time. It contains three computers that make sure it doesn't tumble down stairs or clean the same place twice. This intelligent vacuum cleaner makes 16 decisions every second!

The Smallest Computer Mouse

15 The Cat Eye FinRing is the name of the world's smallest computer mouse. It is manufactured in Taiwan. You wear it on your finger. It has buttons on it just like a larger computer mouse. Each time you rotate your hand, the computer "knows" that the mouse has moved.

The Thinnest Camera

20 The Ultra-Pocket digital camera was made in Massachusetts in the United States. It is only six millimeters thick and weighs only 63.3 grams. It is about the same size as a credit card. It is the thinnest camera in the world.

The Smallest Motorcycle

A Swedish man named Tom Wiberg built the world's smallest motorcycle that can be

25 ridden by a person. The front wheel is 16 millimeters wide, and the back wheel is 22 millimeters wide. The rider sits 65 millimeters above the ground. In 2003 Mr. Wiberg rode his machine for more than ten meters.

E Now, answer the comprehension questions below. Try to answer the questions without looking up the meaning of the unknown word(s) in a dictionary.

1 What is not true about the submarine Shinkai 6500?
   a. It is used only in Japan.
   b. It can dive deeper than other submarines.
   c. Three people can ride in it.
   d. It is 9.5 meters long.

2 Which statement is not true about the Dyson DC06 vacuum cleaner?
   a. It can save you time.
   b. It has more than one computer.
   c. It cleans the same place twice.
   d. It makes 16 decisions a second.

3 How is the Cat Eye FinRing different from all other computer mice?
   a. It has buttons.
   b. The computer "knows" when it moves.
   c. It is made in Taiwan.
   d. You wear it on your finger.

4 What is true about the world's thinnest camera?
   a. It was made in Massachusetts.
   b. It is about the size of a credit card.
   c. It weighs more than 63 grams.
   d. all of the above

5 The world's smallest motorcycle was probably made
   a. for the police.
   b. to sell to Swedish motorcycle riders.
   c. in order to be the smallest in the world.
   d. for Mr. Wiberg to go to work on.

6 What is true about all the machines in the reading?
   a. They are very small.
   b. They have computers.
   c. They are number one in the world in some way.
   d. You can buy them in stores.

Self Check

Write a short answer to each of the following questions.

1. When you read, do you usually try to understand every word?

2. What do you usually do when you find a word you don't know?

3. Do you think that skipping unknown words is helpful?
   Why or why not?

4. Which of the six reading passages in units 7–9 did you enjoy most?
   Why?

5. Which of the six reading passages in units 7–9 was easiest?
   Which was most difficult? Why?

6. What have you read in English outside of class recently?

7. What time of day is the best time for you to read and comprehend
   well? Do you use that part of the day to do your most important
   reading and studying?

8. Are you keeping a vocabulary notebook?

Fluency Practice

Time yourself as you read through the passage. Try to read as fluently as you can. Record your time in the Reading Rate Chart on page 176. Then answer the questions on the following page.

Tips for Business Communication

In the 21st century, more and more business is international. Communication between people of different cultures is more important than ever. Most large companies now understand how important it is
5 to have a knowledge of different cultures and languages. Here is some advice to improve business communication between people of different cultures.

Tip 1: Slow down.
In a business situation, it is very important to communicate your ideas and intentions clearly. Make sure there are no mistakes by speaking clearly and not too fast.

10 ### Tip 2: Take turns.
After each of your statements or questions, wait for the other side to speak. In everyday conversation this can seem strange, but in cross-cultural business situations this formal style makes communication much easier.

Tip 3: Write it down.
15 If you can't clearly understand what someone has said, write it down and check it. This can be very helpful when calculating numbers.

Tip 4: Give encouragement.
It can be very difficult to get the hang of speaking English. If the people you are speaking with are having trouble finding the right words, be sensitive to this. They may need your support.
20 Encourage them not to be shy in communicating.

Tip 5: Use everyday language.
It is usually best not to use informal language or colorful variations of language. These will often not be understood by people from other countries. It is more practical to speak using well-known words and expressions.

25 ### Tip 6: Be careful about jokes.
In many countries, business communication is quite serious and formal. People from other cultures may not be comfortable with jokes in a business situation. Even worse, jokes might be misunderstood or seen as impolite.

280 words   Time taken _____

Reading Comprehension

1 The main idea of this reading is
   a. mistakes that people have made in international communication.
   b. advice for communication between people of different cultures.
   c. the best ways to do business in the 21st century.
   d. how to work for an international company.

2 Which tip would be best for someone who keeps talking all the time?
   a. Tip 1
   b. Tip 2
   c. Tip 3
   d. Tip 4

3 If the other person can't speak English very well, you should
   a. find another person who can speak English better.
   b. give the person encouragement and listen carefully.
   c. tell your boss about it.
   d. write a letter about it to the other company.

4 Which of these is not a reason to be careful about telling jokes?
   a. The jokes might not be understood.
   b. Someone else might tell the same joke.
   c. Jokes aren't always right for formal situations.
   d. Someone might think the joke is impolite.

5 In business meetings with people from other countries, you should
   a. use colorful English words and phrases that you know.
   b. use well-known words and expressions.
   c. use informal language.
   d. always speak better than they do.

6 We learn that it is sometimes useful to write things down when
   a. you don't understand what was said.
   b. the other person is speaking too quickly.
   c. it is the other person's turn.
   d. you want to encourage the other person.

Review Reading 6: Chusok—A Popular Korean Celebration

Fluency Practice

Time yourself as you read through the passage. Try to read as fluently as you can. Record your time in the Reading Rate Chart on page 176. Then answer the questions on the following page.

Chusok
A Popular Korean Celebration

Chusok is one of the most important celebrations in the Korean calendar. Chusok takes place in the eighth month of the lunar calendar (in either September or October), on
5 the night of the full moon. During Chusok, Koreans give thanks and show their respect for nature and for people in the family who have died.

Nowadays, many people have moved away from their hometowns to work in big cities like Seoul. During Chusok, people who have moved away return to their hometowns to
10 celebrate and socialize together. Therefore, the roads are very busy and the government gives everyone a day off work before and after Chusok. Many people use these days for traveling.

The first day is spent traveling or preparing traditional foods for ceremonies and eating. New rice is used to make moon-shaped rice cakes with a sweet filling. They are called
15 songphyun. Other foods are rice, soup, kimchi, fish, meat, fruits, and vegetables of the fall season.

The next day is the day of ceremonies and celebration. People dress in nice clothes. Some dress in hanbok, the traditional clothing of Korea. There are traditional ceremonies in which foods are placed on a table as a sacrifice for people in the family who have died. Everyone
20 in the family enjoys eating and drinking together. Later, traditional games are often played. At night, it is a traditional pleasure to go outdoors under the full moon.

The third day is usually a travel day. People go back to their home, often far from their hometown. Chusok connects Koreans with the past, but it is a celebration everyone enjoys in the present.

270 words   Time taken _____

Reading Comprehension

1 This reading is mainly about
   a. ways that the celebration of Chusok has changed.
   b. what Chusok is and how it is celebrated.
   c. the best ways to celebrate in Korea.
   d. the most popular Korean celebrations.

2 Why does the government give everyone a day off work before and after Chusok?
   a. for returning to their hometowns
   b. for showing respect to people in the family who have died
   c. because government workers want the day off work
   d. because there are three days of celebrations

3 How has Korea changed nowadays?
   a. More people are wearing hanbok.
   b. People now eat songphyun on Chusok.
   c. More people live in big cities.
   d. The rice is new.

4 Which of the following is not part of the Chusok celebrations?
   a. making moon-shaped rice cakes
   b. dressing in nice clothes
   c. going outdoors under the moon
   d. greeting family by saying "Chusok!"

5 Part of a ceremony to remember family members who have died is
   a. placing food on a table.
   b. eating rice, fish, kimchi, fruit, soup, and vegetables.
   c. playing traditional games.
   d. going back home.

6 How does Chusok connect Koreans with the past?
   a. Koreans remember family members who have died.
   b. There are traditions and ceremonies that continue from long ago.
   c. Everyone eats traditional foods.
   d. all of the above

Growing Older

10

VOTE HERE

POLLING PLACE

Getting Ready

Discuss the following questions with a partner.

1 At what age is a person no longer a child?
2 What life events are shown in the pictures above?
3 How old should a person be to do each activity pictured?
4 Which of these have you experienced?

Unit 10   Chapter 1: The Age of Adulthood

Before You Read:
Are You Old Enough?

A Match each word or phrase from the reading with its definition.

1	driver's license	_____	**a.** to play games to win money
2	gamble	_____	**b.** drinks like wine, whisky, and beer
3	nightclub	_____	**c.** the people who fight in a war
4	alcohol	_____	**d.** voting for members of the government
5	army	_____	**e.** a place for late-night drinking and dancing
6	election	_____	**f.** a paper or card that allows you to drive

B Are you old enough for each of these things? How about other people in your family?

Reading Skill:
Predicting

> Before we read, making predictions about the reading can improve our understanding. Good readers naturally ask themselves questions about what they are about to read.

A Discuss the following questions with a partner.

1 Look at the title of the reading on the next page. What do you think "The Age of Adulthood" means?
2 Look at the photograph of the Japanese girl. Why do you think she is dressed up so beautifully in a kimono?
3 The reading talks about important ages for young people in the United States, Latin America, and Japan. What do you think some of those important ages are?

B Skim the reading to see if your ideas in A were correct.

C Read the passage and answer the questions that follow.

The Age of Adulthood

In the United States, sixteen, eighteen, and twenty-one are important ages in a person's life. There are no special celebrations for these birthdays, but each is a time when a person can do new things that show that he or she is no longer a child and has made the **transition** to adulthood.   5

In the United States, after turning sixteen a person can work, get a driver's license,[1] and leave home. Many high school students learn to   10
drive and get part-time jobs soon after celebrating their sixteenth birthday. Sometimes the laws don't seem to **make sense**: at eighteen people in the United States can vote in governmental elections and join the army, but they are **prohibited** from going into many nightclubs, buying drinks like beer or wine, or **gambling** until they are twenty-one.   15

In many Latin American[2] countries, a young woman's fifteenth birthday is important. At this age, she is no longer **considered** to be a girl, but rather a woman. To mark this special day, families with fifteen-year-old daughters have a celebration called a Quinceanera. The day begins with the young woman and her family going to church. Later,   20
there is a party and many guests are invited.

In Japan, boys and girls are considered to be **adults** at the age of twenty. At this age, they are **allowed** by law to vote, drink alcohol, and smoke. The second Monday in January is a national holiday called "Coming of Age Day." On this day, twenty-year-olds celebrate by first going to a   25
shrine[3] with their families. Later, they listen to speeches[4] given by city and school leaders. After that, many celebrate with family or friends late into the night.

In some countries, birthday celebrations continue throughout adulthood. Some people celebrate their fortieth and fiftieth birthdays, or the year   30
that they **retire**, with a big party.

---

[1]**driver's license** a paper or card that allows you to drive a car
[2]**Latin America** Central and South America

[3]**shrine** a religious building
[4]**speech** a talk to a group of people

Reading Comprehension:
Check Your Understanding

A **The statements below are about the reading. Choose the correct answer to complete each one.**

1 The main idea of the reading is _____.
  a. the age of adulthood is too young in some places but too old in others
  b. being a young person in Latin America is easier than in Japan or the United States
  c. there are special ages and celebrations that show a person is growing older

2 Which celebration involves going to church and, later, a party?
  a. the sixteenth birthday   b. Quinceanera   c. Coming of Age Day

3 What do Japanese 20-year-olds do on Coming of Age Day?
  a. listen to speeches   b. drink alcohol   c. go to a nightclub

4 One age you can celebrate that is NOT mentioned in the reading is _____.
  a. your retirement year   b. your fifth birthday   c. your fortieth birthday

B **Decide if the following statements about the reading are true (*T*) or false (*F*). If you check (✓) false, correct the statement to make it true.**

	T	F
1 There are special celebrations for sixteenth, eighteenth, and twenty-first birthdays in the United States.		
2 In many European countries, a young woman's fifteenth birthday is important.		
3 On Coming of Age Day, speeches are given by city and school leaders.		
4 In some countries, some people celebrate their retirement year.		

Critical Thinking

C **Discuss these questions with your partner.**
1 Is becoming an adult only about the age of the person? Explain your ideas.
2 What are some of the things we stop doing when we become adults?

Vocabulary Comprehension:
Words in Context

A **The words in *italics* are vocabulary items from the reading. Read each question or statement and choose the correct answer.**

1 When you *retire*, you _____.
  a. stop working   b. finish celebrating

2 A *transition* is _____.
  a. an ending   b. a change

3 If you are *allowed* to do something, you _____.
  a. can do it   b. have to do it

4 A person becomes an *adult* when he or she _____.
  a. has children   b. is no longer a child

5 It's dangerous to *gamble* because you might _____.

   a. get hurt   **b.** lose your money

6 If you *consider* a question, you _____.

   a. think about it   **b.** solve it

7 If something doesn't *make sense*, it _____.

   a. is very clear   **b.** is hard to understand

8 If drinking alcohol is *prohibited*, you _____.

   a. don't enjoy it   **b.** can't do it

B **Now complete the sentences below using the words from A. Be sure to use the correct form of the word.**

1 In most countries, only _____ are _____ to drink alcohol, smoke, vote, or join the army.

2 I think that the _____ from life as a student to working life is very difficult.

3 My father _____ last year. He really loved his job, so he's a little unhappy.

4 Knives, guns, and even scissors are _____ on the airplane.

A **Read the passage below and circle all of the *trans-* words that you find.**

> ### Happy Landings for Ernesto!
> Last week life didn't look very good for heart transplant patient Ernesto Medina from Spain. He was told six months ago that he would need the operation if he was to survive. He immediately planned to make the transatlantic journey to a hospital in Chicago to have the operation. While he was in transit at JFK airport in New York, he received the news that his new heart had been accidentally transported to another hospital. Ernesto then had to get on a different plane to transport him to the other hospital, where the operation was carried out in time. Ernesto is now recovering from the transplant. His English-speaking wife translated for him as he said, "I feel like a new man—this new heart has transformed my life."

B **Now, match each of the *trans-* words from A with a definition below.**

1 on a journey; on the way to a place _____

2 changed completely _____

3 take, move, or carry something to a place _____

4 to remove an organ from someone's body and place in another person's body _____

5 across the Atlantic Ocean _____

6 to change one language to another _____

Vocabulary Skill:

The Prefix *trans-*

In this chapter, you read the word "transition," a word that uses the prefix "trans-," which means "across," "change," or "move from place to place." "Trans-" comes at the beginning of many words to form nouns, verbs, adjectives, and adverbs in English.

Chapter 2: *Firsts in Life*

Before You Read:
Important Firsts

A Look at this list of important "firsts." Circle any that you can remember in your life. Add one more to the list.

first car	first apartment	first child	first girlfriend/boyfriend
first job	first English class	first pet	first airplane trip

B Choose one of your "firsts" from above and tell a partner about it.

Reading Skill:
Making Inferences

When we make inferences, we think about the reading passage and try to understand more than is written there. When we make inferences, we actively ask questions like, "What does this mean?" or, "Why did he write that?" in order to understand what we read more deeply.

A Scan the article on the next page to find the words in *italics*. Read the paragraph and make inferences about the meaning. Choose the best answer to complete each statement.

1 In line 1, *University Express* is probably _____.
    a. a train   **b.** a magazine   **c.** a television show

2 In line 15, *my best friend's brother*, was Gina's best friend a boy or a girl?
    a. boy   **b.** girl

3 In line 17, *We were both very shy*, they were probably shy because _____.
    a. they didn't know how to dance
    b. they had very little experience with dating
    c. Gina was worried about her friend's brother

4 In line 29, *independent* probably means _____.
    a. disciplined   **b.** practical   **c.** able to do what he wants

B Compare your answers with a partner.

C Read the passage through, then answer the questions that follow.

http://www.ACTIVElife.com

Topic ➩ Firsts in Life

Firsts in Life

In this month's *University Express*, Lynn Zhou **interviews** students around the world about important "firsts" in their lives. Read their answers to the question:

What was an important first in life for you?

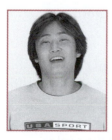

Miguel: For me, an important first was getting my driver's license. In Spain a person can do this at age eighteen. That's when I got mine. Being able to drive my father's car that summer gave me **freedom** and made me feel like an adult. For example, I'm from Madrid, and my girlfriend is from a **suburb** about twenty miles away. Driving made it easy for me to see her more **frequently**. Also, I was able to take weekend trips with friends to other cities.

Gina: I went on my first date soon after my sixteenth birthday with my best friend's brother. He invited me to a movie, but we didn't talk much. We were both very shy. Two weeks later, I went to a high school dance with him, and we had a great time. After that, we spent most of the summer together, but then he and his family moved. I guess you could say he was my first boyfriend.

Soo-Jin: An important first for me was traveling abroad alone from Korea to the United States. When I was seventeen, I spent the summer in New York City studying English. I took a plane to the States by myself. It was my first visit to another country, and I was **frightened**, but **gradually** I **overcame** my fears and learned to be more **independent**. I also made friends from other countries. Now I'm back in the United States, and I'm attending university!

5

10

15

20

25

30

Reading Comprehension:
Check Your Understanding

A Complete the sentences. Write Miguel, Gina, or Soo-Jin.

1 _____ is now living overseas.
2 _____ was invited to a movie and didn't talk much.
3 _____ was able to take weekend trips with friends to other cities.
4 _____ probably speaks English very well.

B Decide if the following statements about the reading are true (*T*) or false (*F*). If you check (✓) false, correct the statement to make it true.

		T	F
1	In Spain, you can get your driver's license at age eighteen.		
2	One important first discussed in the reading was a girl's first boyfriend.		
3	Soo-Jin first went to the United States to go to graduate school.		
4	All of the firsts in the reading took place in the summer.		

Critical Thinking

C Discuss these questions with your partner.
1 Do you think Miguel, Gina, and Soo-Jin have different or similar personalities? How are they different or similar?
2 Do you think that young men and young women have the same idea about what is an important "first"? Why or why not?

Vocabulary Comprehension:
Word Definitions

A Look at the list of words from the reading. Match each word with a definition on the right.

1 freedom _____
2 frequently _____
3 frightened _____
4 gradually _____
5 independent _____
6 interview _____
7 overcome _____
8 suburb _____

a. the power to do what you want
b. not needing the help of other people
c. often
d. to win a fight against people or problems
e. part of a town or city outside the center
f. slowly; little by little
g. afraid; scared
h. to ask a person questions to get information, for example, for a newspaper article

B Now complete the sentences below using the vocabulary from A.
Be sure to use the correct form of the word.

1 I have no intention of moving to a _____; I love the downtown
  area too much!
2 The Americans won their independence when they _____
  the British in 1776.
3 When the reporter _____ the president, he asked him a lot of
  tough questions.
4 Husbands and wives should communicate _____.

A Look at the list of words below that begin with the prefix *sub-*.
Match each word with a definition on the right.

1 submit   _____
2 subtitles   _____
3 subway   _____
4 substitute   _____
5 subsequent   _____
6 submarine   _____

a. words on the bottom of a movie screen that
   translate the actor's words
b. replacement for the first person or thing
c. an underground tunnel or transportation system
d. to hand in some work; to introduce an idea
e. an underwater ship
f. happening later; following on from something

**Vocabulary
Skill:**
The Prefix *sub-*

In this chapter, you
learned the word
"suburb" "Sub-"
is a prefix that
means "under"
or "lower." It
can come at
the beginning
of a noun, verb,
adjective, or
adverb.

B Now use a word from A to complete each sentence below.

1 This city has a variety of transportation systems: electric buses, taxis,
  monorails, and a _____ system.
2 Our government has developed a new kind of _____ that
  can stay under the ocean for one year.
3 We greeted Professor Hartshorn when he entered the room, and
  we _____ our homework assignments to him right away.
4 The teacher in our adult education course was a _____;
  I think our usual teacher was sick.
5 The first letter of ATM stands for "automatic." The _____ two
  letters stand for "teller" and "machine."
6 I don't speak French, so at the French film festival I had to read
  the _____ all the time.

Real Life Skill:
Choosing the Right Word

English has many groups of words that are similar in meaning but are used very differently. A good English language dictionary can explain these differences. Usage notes in dictionaries tell you how and when to use a word.

A Read the following dictionary entry and usage notes.

> **land** /lænd/   **1** soil, earth   **2** area of ground owned as property
> **3** a country or nation

USAGE NOTE:
The Earth's surface when compared with the sea is the **land**:
*After sailing for a month, the sailors saw **land**.*
An area that someone owns as property is a piece of **land**:
*In New York City, **land** is very expensive.*
The substance in which plants grow is **soil** or **earth**. However, **Earth** with a capital *E* means our planet:
*The **soil** in Thailand is good for growing rice. The farmer picked up a handful of **earth**. After a month in space, the astronaut returned to **Earth**.*
Ground means the surface we walk on, but when this is indoors, it is the **floor**:
*When we have a picnic, we sit on the **ground**. When I watch TV, I sit on the **floor**.*

B Complete each sentence below by using *land*, *Earth*, *soil*, *ground*, or *floor*. Use each word once. Explain your choices to a partner.

1 In some countries, people don't sleep in beds. They feel more comfortable sleeping on the _____.

2 I am considering buying a piece of _____ and building my retirement house.

3 While I bathed in the pond, I just left my clothes on the _____.

4 If you look at this pile of _____ you'll see that it contains a lot of sand.

5 Space travel is important, but it's even more important to improve the situation down here on _____.

What Do You Think?

1 What "firsts" do you hope to experience in the future?

2 Imagine you are going to live and work in an English-speaking country. What "firsts" do you think you will experience?

3 When you celebrate "firsts," do you prefer to have a big celebration with lots of people, or just a quiet little party with friends? Explain your reasons.

Look into the Future

Getting Ready

Discuss the following questions with a partner.

1 What are the signs on the chart above used for?
2 Can you name all twelve of the signs?
3 Do you know of any similar ways to describe someone's personality?
4 Do you believe that these ways are helpful? Why or why not?

Unit 11   *Chapter 1: What's Your Sign?*

Before You Read:
Personality

A **What kind of person are these statements about? Match each statement with an adjective.**

1 "She's keeping it all for herself!" _____
2 "She always visits people in the hospital." _____
3 "He's a fast learner." _____
4 "She travels all around the world." _____
5 "He has never had an accident in his life." _____
6 "She never does any work!" _____
7 "I don't think I've ever seen him smile." _____
8 "I fight to get a word in when I'm with her." _____

a. adventurous
b. careful
c. kind
d. lazy
e. selfish
f. serious
g. smart
h. talkative

B **Do any of these adjectives describe you, family members, or friends? Discuss with a partner.**

Reading Skill:
Identifying Main Ideas within Paragraphs

Every paragraph has a main idea. This idea gives us the most important information in that paragraph. Often the first or second sentence of the paragraph gives us the main idea.

A **Scan through the passage quickly. Underline the main idea in each paragraph.**

B **Look at the statements below. Write "M" next to the statement that is the main idea of each paragraph. Share your answers with a partner.**

Paragraph 1
    a. Ancient people studied the stars and created the zodiac.
    b. The zodiac was first used to keep track of time.

Paragraph 2
    a. A person born on March 30 is an Aries.
    b. Some people believe a person's personality is connected to their date of birth.

Paragraph 3
    a. The Chinese zodiac is used in Asia to describe personality and talk about the future.
    b. The animals in the Chinese zodiac stand for different personalities.

Paragraph 4
    a. People with the blood type AB are honest; type Bs are independent.
    b. Blood type is also used in Asia to describe personality.

C **Now read the passage again, then answer the questions that follow.**

What's Your Sign?

Thousands of years ago, the ancient[1] people of Babylon[2] and Egypt studied the stars in the sky and created the zodiac. It was first used to **keep track of** time. Later, many used the stars to describe a person's personality and to say what would happen in the future.

A person's zodiac sign is **connected** to his or her birth date. Some believe this sign can tell us about a person's **personality**. For example, some think that a person born under the sign of Aries (between March 21 and April 20) is adventurous and isn't afraid to **take risks**. A person born under Cancer (between June 22 and July 23) is kind and happiest in the home.

In many countries in Asia, people believe the Chinese zodiac describes personality and can **reveal** the future. In the Chinese zodiac, there are twelve animals. A person's animal sign is connected to his or her birth year. Every animal stands for a different type of personality. People born in the year of the rat are friendly, but careful. Those born in the year of the monkey are smart and good at making money. Many believe that the rat and monkey are a good match.

In Asia, a person's blood type is also used to describe personality. People with the blood type A are calm and serious, but they can be selfish. Type Bs are independent but can be lazy. ABs are honest, and type Os are loving and talkative.

Not everybody believes that your birth sign or blood type describes your personality. In fact, some people **disapprove** of using the zodiac; they say it's just **foolishness**. But, if reading your horoscope[3] **amuses** you, go ahead and read it!

[1]**ancient** very old
[2]**Babylon** a very old city located near what is now Baghdad in Iraq
[3]**horoscope** written description of a person's personality and what will happen in his or her future

Reading Comprehension:
Check Your Understanding

A The statements below are about the reading. Choose the correct answer to complete each one.

1 The main idea of the reading is _____.
  a. to show that the zodiac and blood types can correctly describe personality
  b. to explain how some people try to describe personality and reveal the future
  c. to show that the zodiac and blood types are foolishness

2 The author probably thinks that the zodiac and blood types _____.
  a. are excellent ways to describe personality and reveal the future
  b. can be dangerous if people believe in them
  c. are fun to use whether or not they are true

3 The stars were used to create _____.
  a. the zodiac   b. your date of birth   c. a person's personality

4 Reading your horoscope _____.
  a. can be difficult   b. is dangerous   c. can be fun and enjoyable

B Complete the following statements using the correct words and phrases from the reading.

1 Some people think that a person born under the sign of Aries is _____.

2 A person born under the sign of Cancer is happiest in the _____.

3 In the Chinese zodiac there are _____ animals.

4 People with the blood type O are loving and _____.

Critical Thinking

C Discuss these questions with your partner.

1 Why do some people say that the zodiac is just foolishness?

2 Is it important to check the zodiac before deciding to marry? Why or why not?

Vocabulary Comprehension:
Words in Context

A The words in *italics* are vocabulary items from the reading. Read each question or statement and choose the correct answer.

1 Someone who is *amused* often _____.
  a. laughs   b. asks a question

2 People who *take risks* _____.
  a. do something dangerous to get something they want
  b. know something about the future

3 If you *connect* two things, you _____.
  a. tell how they originated
  b. join them together

4 If someone *disapproves* of an idea they _____.
  a. think it is good   b. don't think it is good

5 A person who is known for his or her *foolishness* is probably not very _____.

   a. funny   **b.** sensible

6 If you *keep track of* the books you read you _____.

   a. give them to your friends   **b.** make a list of them

7 My son's *personality* is just like mine. He's very _____.

   a. tall   **b.** adventurous

8 When you *reveal* some information you _____.

   a. keep it secret   **b.** tell someone about it

B **Answer these questions. Share your answers with a partner.**

1 What are some examples of things that amuse you? _____

2 How have you seen people take risks on television? _____

3 What things are happening in the world that you disapprove of?

   _____

4 What are your favorite types of personalities? _____

A **Look at the adjectives used to describe people in the chart below. Decide if they are positive (+), negative (–), or neutral (=). Then, scan the reading to find an antonym for each word.**

Adjective	+, –, or =	Antonym
unkind	–	kind
unfriendly		
careless		
funny		
generous		
quiet		
dishonest		

Vocabulary Skill:
Antonyms

An antonym is a word that has the opposite meaning of another word; for example, "light" and "dark," "true" and "false." One good way to increase your vocabulary is to learn antonyms.

B **Read the descriptions below. Match an antonym from the chart above with each description.**

1 person who doesn't laugh very much or make jokes _____

2 someone who tells the truth, and whom you can trust _____

3 person who is nice and helpful to other people _____

4 someone who likes to talk a lot _____

5 person who likes to meet and socialize with other people _____

6 someone who takes care when doing things _____

7 person who doesn't share things or think about others _____

Chapter 2: Palm Reading or Hand Reading?

A Look at the photo below. Find the Heart Line, the Head Line, and the Life Line on your own hand. Then read the information below.

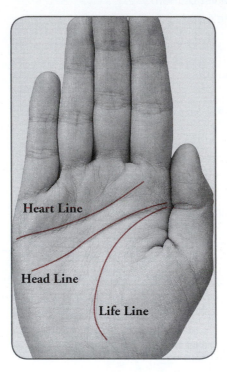

Heart Line

Head Line

Life Line

- A deep Heart Line reveals that family is very important to you. A light Heart Line means that you do not like to be alone.

- A long Head Line reveals that you think very carefully. A short Head Line means you make decisions quickly.

- A person with a deep Life Line likes competition. A light Life Line means you're a thinker rather than a doer.

B Do you agree with what your hand lines revealed about you?

Reading Skill:
Identifying Transition Words

When a writer includes transition words in a passage, these words make connections between ideas clear. When we recognize and understand them, our reading comprehension and speed increase.

A Scan the reading to find these transition words in the letter on the next page. Circle them.

after	furthermore	on the other hand	unlike
but	in short	therefore	then

B How are the transition words used? Write them on the line beside their use.

to show sequence in time (2) _____

to show that something is different (3) _____

to show a result _____

to summarize _____

to add information _____

C Read through the letter again and answer the questions that follow.

Palm Reading or Hand Reading?

To *The Daily News*:

I am writing about your **recent** article, "The Secrets of Reading Palms." It was interesting in some ways, but on the whole it was rather old-fashioned.[1] The palm reading that the article described is, in most people's minds, a kind of fortune-telling. People expect the palm reader to answer questions like, "How many years will I live?" or, "Will I fall in love with a tall, dark, and handsome stranger?" For me, it is difficult to **have confidence** in a palm reader who **claims** to know a person's future simply on the basis of palm lines.

After a short look at my palm, a palm reader once told me that I was honest, smart, not lazy, and not at all selfish! She then said that I would find a love match soon. I wish it were true. I was quite **suspicious**. How could I believe that my past, present, or future can be known from the few lines on the palm of my hand! The lines on the hand often change as we age. Therefore, I believe it doesn't make sense to use these changing lines to make judgments about a person's life and personality.

On the other hand, the article doesn't even consider the modern[2] field of hand reading. Unlike old-fashioned palm readers, modern hand readers **take into account** the entire hand and body. Furthermore, hand readers need to be knowledgeable in the art of acupuncture.[3] Through experience of many hands, it is possible to understand a person's personality, **stress** level, as well as strengths and **weaknesses**. They can tell us things about ourselves that we didn't know, and this can be very useful in improving our lives. In short, I think they **deserve** to be listened to.

Very truly yours,

Sunil Jaiswal

Sunil Jaiswal

[1] **old fashioned** not new; like things used in the past
[2] **modern** very new
[3] **acupuncture** a kind of Chinese medicine

Reading Comprehension:
Check Your Understanding

A The statements below are all about the reading. Choose the correct answer to complete each one.

1 The main idea of the letter is to say that _____.
   a. it's not possible to know about someone's personality from their hands
   b. most palm readers do not tell the truth
   c. hand reading is better than palm reading at helping to understand personality
2 The reason Sunil Jaiswal wrote this letter to *The Daily News* is _____.
   a. he enjoyed reading a recent article about palm reading
   b. he disagreed with a recent article they printed
   c. he hopes they will ask him to write letters more often
3 The writer thinks that hand reading is _____.
   a. suspicious   b. useful   c. changing
4 Hand readers look at _____.
   a. the whole body   b. just the hands   c. just the palms

B Are the following statements about the letter writer's ideas true (*T*) or false (*F*)? If you check (✓) false, correct the statement.

		T	F
1	In some ways, the article "The Secrets of Reading Palms" was interesting.		
2	People expect a palm reader to answer questions like, "What college will I attend?"		
3	The lines on the palm stay the same as we age.		
4	Hand readers can tell us things about ourselves that we don't already know.		

Critical Thinking

C Discuss these questions with your partner.
   1 Why did Sunil Jaiswal think it was important to write to *The Daily News*?
   2 Do you think it is possible to know about the future? If no, why not? If yes, what is the best way to learn about the future?

Vocabulary Comprehension:
Word Definitions

A Look at the list of words from the reading. Match each word with a definition on the right.

1 claim   _____   a. to feel sure about
2 have confidence in _____   b. not trusting or believing
3 deserve   _____   c. not being strong
4 recent   _____   d. to say that something is true
5 stress   _____   e. be good enough to have something
6 suspicious   _____   f. a feeling of worry

7 take into account _____

8 weakness _____

g. that happened a short time ago

h. to think about something when making a decision

B **Now complete the sentences below using the vocabulary from A. Be sure to use the correct form of the word.**

1 I don't have confidence in the new president. I'm _____ that he might not care about the country.

2 To be healthy, you not only have to think about food and sleep. You need to _____ stress as well.

3 That crazy doctor _____ that smoking cigarettes actually makes you live longer!

4 When I was young I never attended the spring festival, but in _____ years I've never missed one.

A **Add the suffix -ness to the adjectives in the box to form nouns. Use the nouns to complete the sentences below. For adjectives of more than one syllable that end in -y, change y to i before adding -ness.**

> awesome   foolish   shy   good
> happy   sad   useful   weak

1 Neither gold, nor silver, nor all the money in the world is more valuable than _____.

2 The _____ of Mother Theresa of Calcutta was very clear to the thousands of street people that she helped.

3 You can only really appreciate the _____ of Mount Everest by climbing it.

4 My brother isn't strong enough to stop gambling even though he loses lots of money. For him, gambling is a real _____.

5 Our family experienced a lot of _____ after our pet cat Felix died.

6 My brother is in high school, and he still can't talk to girls. He can't seem to overcome his _____.

7 Don't bother listening to that guy talking on the street corner. Everything he says is _____.

8 The _____ of the wheel has shown itself in all types of ground transportation.

B **Write the noun form of each of these adjectives. Not all of them use the suffix -ness. Use your dictionary to help you.**

1 formal _____

2 valuable _____

3 flashy _____

4 forgetful _____

5 curious _____

6 loud _____

7 convenient _____

8 open _____

Vocabulary Skill:

The Suffix -ness

> The suffix "-ness" is used to change certain adjectives into nouns. When we add the suffix "-ness" to the adjective "foolish," the adjective becomes the noun "foolishness."

Real Life Skill:
Doing Research on the Internet

Searching the Internet is an important skill. Even if you can't understand all the writing on a website, your scanning skills can guide you to the information you want.

A Read about the practice of reading tea leaves.

Reading tea leaves is an ancient practice that began in China. Most people do not take it very seriously anymore, but it is still very interesting. Reading tea leaves can even be found in Harry Potter books.

After drinking a cup of tea with leaves in it, you turn the cup upside down and drop the leaves on a dish. The tea-leaf reader looks at the leaves and, using his or her imagination, sees many different shapes. Each shape is a symbol and it has meaning.

B Do an Internet search using the search words *tea leaf symbols*. Write the meaning of each of the symbols in the list.

Symbols	Meanings
baby	
bird	
boat	
car	
circle	
clock	
coin	
dish	
grapes	
hand	
hat	
heart	
knife	
spoon	
tree	
triangle	

C Compare the meanings you found with another student.

What Do You Think?

1 What would you most like to know about your future?
2 Can you remember a prediction about the future that came true? What was it? Who made it?
3 What are some things that you think are going to happen in the future in your life?
4 What are some events that you think are going to happen in the world?

Folk Tales and Hoaxes

Getting Ready

Discuss the following questions with a partner.

1 Above are some scenes from a very famous folk tale. Do you know the name of it?
2 What is happening in each of the scenes?
3 Folk tales are stories that come to us from long, long ago. What are some of your country's folk tales?
4 What are some of the things that folk tales can teach us?

Chapter 1: The Greedy Innkeeper

Before You Read:
Special Foods and Drinks

Before You Read:
Special Foods and Drinks

A In the story on the next page, *ginger buds* are a food that some people think can make a person forgetful. How do other foods and drinks make you feel? Write examples in the chart.

Foods and drinks that . . .	Examples
can make you fat	
make you stronger	
make you sleepy	
wake you up	
make you smarter	
make you happy	

B Compare your examples with a partner. If you agree with your partner's examples, write them in your chart.

Reading Skill:
Recognizing Sequence of Events

> In reading passages that are organized according to a sequence of events, it is very important for us to understand which events come first, second, etc. Words such as "first," "then," or "after" can help us to know the order of events.

A These events are from the story on the next page. Without reading the story, number them in the correct order. Circle the words that helped you choose the correct order. Compare your answers with a partner.

___ "Delicious!" said the rich man.

___ In the morning, the innkeeper saw the rich man off at the front door.

_1_ One day, a rich man stopped at an inn.

___ Soon, the rich man descended the stairs and requested dinner.

___ The rich man requested the most expensive room at the inn.

___ Then he went upstairs to dress for dinner.

___ When dinner was finished, he went to bed happy and full of ginger buds.

B Quickly skim the story. Compare the events in the reading with the order of events in your time line above.

C Read the passage again and answer the questions that follow.

The Greedy Innkeeper

Once upon a time, in a beautiful mountain inn,[1] there was a **greedy** old innkeeper[2] who was always thinking about money.

One day, a rich man stopped at the inn. The innkeeper looked at the guest's fat money belt and she thought, "Oh, if only all that money could be mine!" The rich man **requested** the most expensive room at the inn, and he went up to his room to dress for dinner.   5

Now, all around the inn there grew beautiful Japanese ginger plants. Many people say that eating buds[3] of ginger makes a person forgetful. This gave the innkeeper an idea.

"This evening for dinner I'll serve ginger bud tempura![4]" she thought. "Then,   10 when the rich man leaves in the morning, he'll be forgetful and leave his money belt behind!" She ran into the kitchen and started cooking up the most delicious ginger bud tempura she had ever made.

Soon, the rich man **descended** the **stairs** and requested dinner. The innkeeper could hardly contain her **delight** as she served him **dish** after dish of ginger   15 buds. "Delicious!" said the rich man. When dinner was finished, he went to bed happy and full of ginger buds.

In the morning, the innkeeper saw the rich man off at the front door. As soon as he was out of sight, she raced up to his room. She looked all over the room for the money belt, but she couldn't find it. **Suddenly**, she noticed a piece of   20 paper on the floor. It was the rich man's bill. He had forgotten to pay it! She ran down the stairs, out the front door, and up the road until she was **out of breath**, but the rich man was already far, far away.

---

[1]**inn** a small, country-style hotel
[2]**innkeeper** the manager of an inn

[3]**buds** flowers before they open
[4]**tempura** a style of Japanese cooking

Reading Comprehension:

Check Your
Understanding

A **The following statements are all about the reading. Complete each one using the correct words or phrases.**

1 What does the author want us to learn from this story?
   a. Innkeepers are always thinking about money.
   b. Trying to take things that belong to others is foolish.
   c. If you ever stay at a country inn, be careful about your money.
2 The story of The Greedy Innkeeper _____.
   a. is probably just a story and never happened
   b. probably happened a long time ago
   c. is probably true but has been changed a little
3 After he left the inn, the rich man was probably _____.
   a. very angry at the innkeeper
   b. feeling lucky that he didn't lose his money
   c. not aware that anything had happened
4 The piece of paper on the floor was _____.
   a. a note from the rich man
   b. a bill for the room at the inn
   c. a piece of writing paper

B **Read the statements below. Do you think they are true (*T*) or false (*F*)? Check (✓) the correct box.**

		T	F
1	The rich man stopped at the inn because he knew there was excellent ginger bud tempura there.		
2	The rich man changed his clothes before dinner.		
3	The rich man knew that the innkeeper wanted his money belt.		
4	The innkeeper ran after the rich man because she wanted his money belt.		

Critical Thinking

C **Discuss these questions with your partner.**

1 How do you feel about the rich man forgetting to pay his bill?
2 Do you think Japanese ginger buds really make people forgetful?
3 Most people think this is a funny story. Do you think this is so? Why or why not?

Vocabulary Comprehension:

Odd Word Out

A **For each group, circle the word or phrase that does not belong. The words in *italics* are vocabulary items from the reading.**

1 *descend*   fall   improve
2 tired   *out of breath*   frightened

3	*delight*	disapproval	excitement
4	plate	*dish*	flag
5	independent	free	*greedy*
6	*request*	deserve	ask
7	elevator	*stairs*	festival
8	*suddenly*	unexpectedly	gradually

B Complete the sentences using the words in *italics* from A. Be sure to use the correct form of the word.

1 Leila is _____ because she ran all the way home.

2 John _____ the mountain on skis.

3 If you need more money, make a formal _____ to the boss.

4 The _____ man frequently counted his money.

A Look at some examples of how adverbs are formed.

Many adverbs are formed by adding -*ly* to the end of an adjective.
The dog made a sudden movement.   The dog suddenly moved.

When adjectives end in -*le*, we change the *e* to a *y*.
This chair is very comfortable.   Are you sitting comfortably?

When adjectives end in -*y*, we change the *y* to an *i* and add -*ly*.
The greedy woman looked at the money belt.
The woman greedily looked at the money belt.

B Write the adverb form of these adjectives.

Adjective	Adverb		Adjective	Adverb
1 beautiful	_____		5 loud	_____
2 legal	_____		6 curious	_____
3 usual	_____		7 nice	_____
4 probable	_____		8 hungry	_____

C Complete the following sentences using either an adjective or an adverb.

1 I never noticed until Coming of Age Day how _____ Chiaki is!

2 For 16-year-olds, drinking alcohol is _____ prohibited.

3 My father _____ disapproves of everything I do.

4 When Jinsong stayed at my house, he was a really _____ guest.

5 We adults are very _____ about what young people think.

6 Fred and Martin shouted _____ at Tony.

Vocabulary Skill:
Adverbs

In this chapter, we saw the words "hardly" and "suddenly." These are examples of adverbs. Adverbs can be used to describe verbs in a sentence; they tell us how something is done.

Chapter 2: Internet Hoaxes

Before You Read:
Believe It or Not!

An Internet hoax is when people use the Internet to try to fool other people and make them believe that something false is really true. These hoaxes are usually harmless jokes.

A Which of these statements do you think are true? Which do you think are hoaxes? Check (✓) your choice.

		True	Hoax
1	A man in Canada owned a cat that weighed 40 kilograms.		
2	There is an island called "Dog Island" where 2,500 dogs live in freedom without owners.		
3	A monkey named Marty can type fluently in English.		
4	There is a website that can send food smells to your computer through the Internet.		
5	Kittens are grown in bottles and their bodies look like bottles.		
6	Companies will pay you to advertise on your body with tattoos.		

B Compare your answers with a partner. The answers are at the bottom of the next page.

Reading Skill:
Identifying Cause and Effect

One relationship between two ideas in a text is cause and effect. The cause can come before or after the effect in the text. The event that happened first is usually the cause. Making a sentence with "because" can help show the cause. The idea that follows "because" is the cause; for example, I can't sleep (effect) because I drank too much coffee (cause).

A Look at the following pairs of sentences. Which is the *cause*, and which is the *effect*? Write C or E beside each.

Paragraph 2
1 The rabbit was hurt. _____ The man helped the rabbit. _____
2 The rabbit was under the house. _____ A cat attacked the rabbit. _____

Paragraph 3
3 There was a hurricane. _____ New Orleans was flooded. _____
4 People were afraid. _____
A photo of a giant crocodile was sent around the Internet. _____

Paragraph 4
5 You send the e-mail to one person. _____ You receive $5.00. _____

B Scan paragraphs 2, 3, and 4 to find the causes and effects mentioned above. Then read those parts of the text carefully to see if your ideas were correct.

C Now read the whole passage, and answer the questions that follow.

ABOUT INTERNET HOAXES | MORE INFO | CONTACT US

The Internet is full of false information. It is important for us all to **avoid** being fooled by such information. Here are three examples of Internet **hoaxes**.

On his website, a man has requested gifts of money to save the life of a pretty little rabbit named Toby that he **rescued** from under his house. 5 A cat must have attacked the rabbit, the man claimed, so he took it

in. He gave Toby loving care and **nursed** him back to health. There is a very **cruel** point, however. If the greedy man doesn't receive enough money, he will eat poor little Toby. (Don't worry, though. Remember, it's just a hoax!)

10

While the streets of New Orleans were still flooded after a **terrible** hurricane, a frightening e-mail was sent around the Internet. It 15 included a photograph of an **immense** crocodile over five meters long. According to the message, it had been swimming around the flooded city eating people. It was later discovered that the photographs of the crocodile were of one that was caught in the Congo¹ years before.

20

The following e-mail hoax **takes in** many people. It claims that a large company will pay you to send their e-mail to as many people as possible. For every person that you send the e-mail to, it promises you 25

will receive $5.00; for every person that you send it to that sends it to someone else, you'll get $3.00; and for every third person that receives it, you will be paid $1.00. To make the lie even more believable, the 30 sender says that at first he thought it was a hoax, but the company soon sent him $800.00.

¹**the Congo** an area in Africa

˙sǝxɐoɥ ʇǝuɹǝʇuI llɐ ǝɹɐ ʎǝɥ⊥ :∀ ǝsᴉɔɹǝxƎ oʇ sɹǝʍsu∀

Reading Comprehension:
Check Your Understanding

A The statements below are about the reading. Choose the correct answer to complete each one.

1 The main idea of this reading is _____.
   a. to tell people to be careful of Internet hoaxes and to describe a few of them
   b. to show how anyone can create an Internet hoax
   c. to explain that, even thought they seem false, Internet hoaxes might be true.
2 Toby is the name of a _____.
   a. website   b. man   c. rabbit
3 The crocodile in the photograph was from _____.
   a. New Orleans   b. the Internet   c. the Congo
4 Some people believe they can make money if they _____.
   a. send e-mails   b. receive e-mails   c. read e-mails

B Decide if the following statements about the reading are true (*T*) or false (*F*). If you check (✓) false, correct the statement to make it true.

		T	F
1	Toby the rabbit is really going to die.		
2	The city of New Orleans was really flooded.		
3	The crocodile ate several people.		
4	Someone really received $800 for sending e-mails.		

Critical Thinking

C Discuss these questions with your partner.
1 Do you think the creator of the hoax about Toby the rabbit is probably a bad person? Why or why not?
2 Do you think most people in New Orleans believed the crocodile hoax at first? Why or why not?
3 How can you know if an e-mail offer is a lie?

Vocabulary Comprehension:
Word Definitions

A Look at the list of words from the reading. Match each word with a definition on the right.

1 avoid _____
2 cruel _____
3 immense _____
4 hoax _____
5 nurse _____
6 rescue _____
7 take in _____
8 terrible _____

a. unkind
b. very bad
c. to help get someone or something out of danger
d. false information meant to fool people
e. very big
f. try not to let something happen
g. to help a sick person or animal get healthy
h. to fool

B Now complete the sentences below using the vocabulary from A. Be sure to use the correct form of the word.

1 That man has a _____ personality. He's always unkind to animals.

2 Some people are amused when others are _____ by hoaxes.

3 The movie star didn't want to talk and _____ every interview.

4 Oil is transported in _____ ships called tankers.

A Look at this list of nouns that are also verbs. Can you add any more to the list?

water	mask	compliment
mail	host	light
stamp	salt	phone
cover	support	vote
_____	_____	_____

Vocabulary Skill:
Nouns That Are Also Verbs

Over time, some nouns become verbs in English. This ancient process is called "verbing." Some of the older products of "verbing" are "salt" and "mail," while newer ones are "blog" and "gift." Some people disapprove of making new verbs out of nouns, but it happens frequently anyway.

B In each of these sentences, replace the phrase in parentheses with the correct form of a verb from A.

1 Martha, will you please (pour water on) ___*water*___ the plants during my vacation?

2 Stan is always (giving compliments to) _____ Leslie. I think he likes her.

3 The police always allow you to (make a phone call to) _____ someone.

4 Please consider (casting your vote) _____ for Sue Kennedy for president.

5 Mel (was the host at) _____ a really big party last night. It was a nice chance for new students to socialize.

6 During the winter, my father (puts a cover on) _____ our swimming pool.

7 Although it was night, the moon (shined light on) _____ our way to the beach.

8 I've already (put salt in) _____ the soup, so you don't add any more.

Real Life Skill:

Understanding Internet Abbreviations and Emoticons

Many abbreviations are used in chat rooms and in e-mail in order to save time. FYI (for your information) and CU (see you) are examples of these. Because we cannot see the face of the person we are writing to, emoticons are used instead of facial expressions. Examples of emoticons are :-) (a smiling face) or ;-) (a winking face).

A Match these Internet abbreviations with their meanings.

1	ASAP _____	**a.**	no problem
2	BTW _____	**b.**	boyfriend
3	FYI _____	**c.**	keep in touch
4	IMO _____	**d.**	as soon as possible
5	KIT _____	**e.**	laughs out loud
6	LOL _____	**f.**	in my opinion
7	NP _____	**g.**	girlfriend
8	TY _____	**h.**	for your information
9	G/F _____	**i.**	thank you
10	B/F _____	**j.**	by the way

B Now match these emoticons with their meanings.

Emoticons		Meanings
_____ 1	:-) or (^_^)	**a.** crying
_____ 2	;-) or (^_~)	**b.** thinking about money
_____ 3	:-(or (<_>)	**c.** singing
_____ 4	T_T or (;_;)	**d.** dead
_____ 5	:-o or (O_O)	**e.** winking
_____ 6	($_$)	**f.** surprised
_____ 7	(^o^)	**g.** sad
_____ 8	(x_x)	**h.** happy

C **E-mail Challenge:** Send a partner an e-mail message. Use any of the abbreviations and emoticons above, or others that you know.

What Do You Think?

1 Are you the kind of person who believes things easily? Why or why not?
2 Are folk tales mostly for children, or are they for adults, too?
3 Why do some people create Internet hoaxes?
4 Do you think there should be some punishment for people who create Internet hoaxes in some cases? Why or why not, and in which cases?

Review Unit 4

Fluency Strategy: *Reading ACTIVEly*

In order to become a more fluent reader, remember to follow the six points of the **ACTIVE** approach—before, while, and after you read. See the inside front cover for more information on the **ACTIVE** approach.

Activate Prior Knowledge

Before you read, it's important to think about what you already know about the topic, and what you want to get out of the text.

A Look at the passage on the next page. Read only the title and look at the picture. What do you think the article is about? What kinds of things might people be too young for?

_____

B Now read the first sentence of the passage. What do you know about this topic? In your country, what are the ages at which a person can drink alcohol or get married? Do you agree with these laws? Discuss with a partner.

Cultivate Vocabulary

As you read, you may come across unknown words. Remember, you don't need to understand all the words in a passage to understand the meaning of the passage. Skip the unknown words for now, or guess at their meaning and come back to them later. Note useful new vocabulary in your vocabulary notebook—see page 6 for more advice on vocabulary.

A Now read the first paragraph of the passage. Circle any words or phrases you don't know. Can you understand the rest of the paragraph even if you don't understand those items?

B Write the unknown words here. Without using a dictionary, try to guess their meaning. Use the words around the unknown word and any prefixes, suffixes, or word roots to help you.

New word/phrase   I think it means:

_____   _____

_____   _____

Think About Meaning

As you read, think about what you can infer, or "read between the lines," for example about the author's intention, attitudes, and purpose for writing.

Read the opening paragraph again and discuss these questions with a partner.

- Do you think this article was written by an old or a young person? Where do you think the person lives?
- Why do you think this writer wrote the article? Where might you find this piece of writing?
- What do you think the author means by "should be changed"? Should the age be lowered or raised?

Increase Reading Fluency

To increase your reading fluency, it's important to monitor your own reading habits as you read. Look again at the tips on page 8. As you read, follow these tips.

Now read the whole passage, "How Young Is Too Young?" As you read, check your predictions from "Think About Meaning."

How Young Is Too Young?

I don't agree with laws concerning ages of drinking alcohol, driving, gambling, and marriage in the United States. These laws about young people's freedom don't make sense and are too inconsistent—they really vary from place to place. I think many should be changed.

5 In 1984 the United States government passed a law that set the legal age for drinking alcohol at 21. I don't agree with this. I consider a person to be an adult at 18. I think 18 should be the legal drinking age.

The legal voting age used to be 21, but now it is 18, and I hope it will gradually move even lower. Young people shouldn't be prohibited from choosing their

10 leaders. I think anyone who wants to vote should be allowed to.

The legal ages for driving and gambling don't make sense, because they are different from place to place. In many states the driving age is 16, in others 15, while in Hawaii it is 18. The gambling age is 21 in Colorado, 18 in New York, and 16 in Maine. I can't understand the reason for these variations.

15 The legal age of marriage is 18, except for Nebraska where it is 19 and Mississippi where it is 21. In Iran, the age for men is 15 and women 13, while in Senegal it is 20 for men and 16 for women. I don't understand why it is necessary to set an age at all.

Finally, I think young people should work together to address

20 this situation. Write to your leaders in the government and let them know how you feel!

Verify Strategies

To build your reading fluency, it's important to be aware of how you use strategies to read, and to consider how successfully you are using them.

Use the questions in the Self Check on the next page to think about your use of reading strategies.

Evaluate Progress

Evaluating your progress means thinking about how much you understood from the passage, and how fluently you were able to read the passage to get the information you needed.

Check how well you understood the passage by answering the following questions.

1 This reading is mainly about
   a. the ages at which various activities are allowed by law.
   b. why many legal ages don't make sense and should be changed.
   c. how young people can lower the legal ages.
   d. how different United States laws are from those of other countries.

2 The writer of the passage thinks that the legal drinking age should be 18 because
   a. at that age a person is considered to be an adult.
   b. at 21 people are too old to drink.
   c. it will move even lower in the future.
   d. the United States passed a law in 1984.

3 In the United States, different states have different legal ages for
   a. voting.
   b. drinking alcohol.
   c. passing laws.
   d. marriage.

4 The writer of the passage believes that 18 should be the legal age for
   a. drinking alcohol.
   b. voting.
   c. gambling.
   d. getting married.

5 For whom is the legal age of marriage the youngest?
   a. men in Mississippi
   b. women in Senegal
   c. women in Iran
   d. women in Nebraska

6 We learn that
   a. legal ages are sometimes changed.
   b. leaders never listen to young people.
   c. most countries have the same legal ages.
   d. the reasons for legal ages are easy to understand.

Self Check

A Here is a list of all the reading skills in Active Skills for Reading Book 1. For each skill, say whether you found the skill useful, not useful, or if you need more work with it. Check (✔) the correct box.

Reading skill	Useful	Not useful	Needs work
Distinguishing Main Idea and Supporting Details			
Identifying Cause and Effect			
Identifying Main Ideas			
Identifying Main Ideas within Paragraphs			
Identifying Supporting Details			
Identifying Transition Words			
Making Inferences			
Predicting			
Reading for Details			
Recognizing Sequence of Events			
Scanning			
Skimming for Main Ideas			
Using Subtitles to Predict Content			

B Here are the four fluency strategies covered in the Review Units. For each strategy, say whether you found it useful, not useful, or if you need more work with it. Check (✔) the correct box.

Fluency strategy	Useful	Not useful	Needs work
SQ3R			
KWL			
Dealing with Unknown Words			
Reading ACTIVEly			

C Look again at the *Are You an Active Reader?* quiz on page 10 and complete your answers again. How has your reading fluency improved since you started this course?

Review Reading 7: Zodiac Profiles

Fluency Practice

Time yourself as you read through the passage. Try to read as fluently as you can. Record your time in the Reading Rate Chart on page 176. Then answer the questions on the following page.

www.asrinformation.com/zodiac

Aries 3/21–4/19
Aries personalities are adventurous and not afraid to take risks. They go after what they want, even if others disapprove. They love travel and freedom. They are usually lots of fun. On the other hand, they also give their friends a lot of stress.

5 ### Taurus 4/20–5/20
Taurus personalities are extremely strong and don't change easily. Therefore, they are good family people. Unlike Aries, Taurus is happy to stay home. They are people you can have confidence in.

Virgo 8/23–9/22
10 For Virgo personalities, work is important. They always keep track of what needs to be done. They commonly take work home. After work, many Virgos go to the health club to work on their bodies.

Libra 9/23–10/22
Libra personalities think of others before they think of themselves. Therefore, they
15 are great "team players." They sacrifice their own pleasure so that others can be happy.

Scorpio 10/23–11/21
Scorpio personalities are the most curious of the zodiac. They try to find out others' deepest secrets. Then, they may never show their true feelings about what they
20 found out, so it's OK to be a little suspicious around them.

Capricorn 12/22–1/19
Like Virgos, Capricorn personalities are great workers. Work comes first in their lives. Unfortunately, their lives can easily become all work and no play, and they might sometimes seem not to care about other people's feelings.

25 ### Pisces 2/19–3/20
Pisces personalities love to dream. They often use art to express their deep feelings. They are not very practical people, especially when they are under stress. They are good listeners.

280 words   Time taken _____

Reading Comprehension

1 The zodiac profiles in the reading are about
   a. what people will become.
   b. different types of personalities.
   c. what will happen to people in the future.
   d. different things people need to do.

2 What is the zodiac sign of a person born on January 1?
   a. Libra
   b. Scorpio
   c. Capricorn
   d. Pisces

3 Which two signs seem to like to work a lot?
   a. Aries and Virgo
   b. Taurus and Scorpio
   c. Virgo and Capricorn
   d. Capricorn and Pisces

4 Which sign seems to be the least selfish?
   a. Aries
   b. Taurus
   c. Virgo
   d. Libra

5 Which sign seems to be the most serious?
   a. Aries
   b. Libra
   c. Capricorn
   d. Pisces

6 Why might Capricorn personalities not seem to care about other people's feelings?
   a. They hide their true feelings.
   b. They aren't patient.
   c. They are suspicious.
   d. They think too much about work.

Review Reading 8: *Three Centuries of Hoaxes*

Time yourself as you read through the passage. Try to read as fluently as you can. Record your time in the Reading Rate Chart on page 176. Then answer the questions on the following page.

Three Centuries of Hoaxes

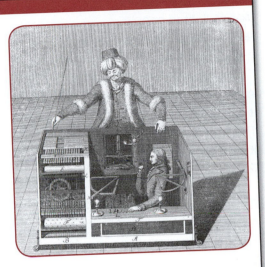

In 1769, long before computers were invented, a man from Hungary built a wonderful machine that could play chess very well indeed. It delighted people all over Europe and beat nearly
5   everyone it played. Many people believed that it was truly a thinking machine. However, other people thought it was a hoax. The secret of the machine was finally revealed in 1837. An article explained that there was a man, who carefully
10 avoided being seen, inside the machine playing chess.

On November 9, 1874, an article in an important New York newspaper claimed that all the animals in the New York Zoo had suddenly escaped and were running all over the city. It also said that there were 27 people dead and 200 harmed. It said the police were working to rescue people from the terrible situation. The entire city of New York was terrified, but
15 there was really no reason to be frightened. The article was a cruel hoax from beginning to end.

On April 21, 1980, the first woman to cross the finish line of the Boston Marathon was 23-year-old Rosie Ruiz. However, as she climbed the stairs to receive her prize, people started to become suspicious because she didn't even seem to be out of breath. None of
20 the other runners remembered seeing her, and her picture never appeared in photographs or TV broadcasts of the race. Later, several people revealed that they had seen her join the race near the very end. She had run only one half of a mile! Her prize was taken away, of course.

270 words   Time taken _____

Reading Comprehension

1 The main idea of the reading is
   a. embarrassing news from the past.
   b. false stories that fooled many people.
   c. how the truth about hoaxes is revealed.
   d. the best ways to fool people.

2 What is true about all the hoaxes in the reading?
   a. They frightened people.
   b. They delighted people.
   c. They made people suspicious.
   d. They fooled a lot of people.

3 What was the secret of the chess-playing machine?
   a. It could play chess very well.
   b. There was someone inside it.
   c. It delighted people.
   d. People thought it was a hoax.

4 How many people were really killed by zoo animals in New York on November 9, 1874?
   a. None
   b. 15
   c. 27
   d. 200

5 Which of the following is not mentioned in the reading as a reason people became suspicious of Rosie Ruiz?
   a. She didn't seem to be out of breath.
   b. Her prize was taken away.
   c. The other runners didn't remember seeing her.
   d. She didn't appear in TV broadcasts of the race.

6 We learn that hoaxes
   a. are not something new.
   b. are easily avoided.
   c. are always cruel.
   d. usually frighten people.

Vocabulary Index

Unit 1
Chapter 1

collect /kəˈlekt/ v. to come or bring together as a group: *The teacher collected the homework.*

encourage /ɪnˈkɜːrɪdʒ/ v. to give strength or hope: *She encouraged her son to go to college.*

gain weight /geɪn weɪt/ *expression* to go up, increase: *He gained a lot of weight this winter.*

harmful /ˈhɑːrmfəl/ *adj.* able to cause hurt or damage: *Smoking cigarettes can be harmful to your health.*

healthy /ˈhelθi/ *adj.* in good health: *His wife had a healthy baby boy.*

kitchen /ˈkɪtʃɪn/ n. a room where you can prepare food, and usually find a stove, sink, and refrigerator: *She is cooking in the kitchen.*

serve /sɜːrv/ v. to give food and drink: *He served Italian food at his party.*

simple /ˈsɪmpəl/ *adj.* without many details, not complex: *I drew a simple map.*

_____ _____

_____ _____

Chapter 2

add /æd/ v. to increase the size or amount of something: *We added a room to our house.*

cool /kuːl/ v. not warm or cold, but more cold than hot: *San Francisco has a cool climate.*

cover /ˈkʌvə/ v. to put something on or over something else: *She covered the table with a cloth.*

cut /kʌt/ v. to divide into pieces or parts with a knife: *She cut the apple pie into six pieces.*

fill /fɪl/ v. to use all available space: *Children filled the hole with sand.*

form /fɔːrm/ v. to shape or make an object: *She formed a dish from clay.*

mix /mɪks/ v. to stir together: *I mixed the milk*

and the flour to make bread.

spread /spred/ v. to cover a surface by pushing something all over it: *Spread some butter on the bread.*

_____ _____

_____ _____

Unit 2
Chapter 1

beat /biːt/ v. to win: *Our team beat the other team.*

competition /ˌkɑːmpɪˈtɪʃən/ n. an organized event in which people try to do something better than everyone else: *She is an excellent runner, and she enters every competition that she can.*

curious /ˈkjʊriəs/ *adj.* interested in knowing about things: *I am curious; where did you buy that dress from?*

invite /ɪnˈvaɪt/ v. to ask someone to come to an event: *I invited my friends to a birthday party.*

joke /dʒoʊk/ n. something you do or say that is funny: *I laughed when I heard the joke.*

machine /məˈʃiːn/ n. a device made of separate parts that uses power to do work: *A car is a machine used for transportation.*

smell /smel/ n. odor, scent, aroma: *The smell of soup cooking on the stove made me hungry.*

support /səˈpɔːrt/ n. the act of supporting someone: *Can we have your support at the next meeting?*

_____ _____

_____ _____

Chapter 2

during /ˈdʊrɪŋ/ *prep.* for all the time of: *We took shelter in a store during the thunderstorm.*

keep in touch /kiːp ɪn tʌtʃ/ *expression* to stay in contact: *My high school friends and I still keep in touch.*

opinion /əˈpɪnjən/ n. what someone believes, something not proven in fact: *His opinion is* *that life on earth will improve next year.*

sick /sɪk/ *adj.* not well physically, ill: *He is sick with the flu.*

surely /ˈʃʊrli/ *adv.* certainly, without doubt: *Surely, you don't believe that nonsense.*

temperature /ˈtempərətʃər/ *n.* the degree of heat or cold: *The temperature outside is cold today.*

useful /ˈjuːsfəl/ *adj.* helpful, handy: *Tools, such as a hammer and saw, are useful when you want to fix something.*

vote /voʊt/ *v.* to put "yes" or "no" beside a politician's name or "for" or "against" an idea: *I voted for Franklin Roosevelt for president.*

_____ _____

_____ _____

Unit 3
Chapter 1

abroad /əˈbrɔːd/ *adv.* out of the country: *Our company ships farm machinery abroad.*

comfortable /ˈkʌmfərtəbəl/ *adj.* relaxed and restful: *I sat on the big, soft sofa and made myself comfortable.*

culture /ˈkʌltʃər/ *n.* the ideas, activities (art, foods, businesses), and ways of behaving that are special to a country, people, or region: *In North American culture, men do not kiss men when meeting each other. They shake hands.*

excellent /ˈeksələnt/ *adj.* very high in quality: *The violinist gave an excellent performance; everyone applauded loudly.*

exciting /ɪkˈsaɪtɪŋ/ *adj.* making someone feel delight: *I think rock concerts are exciting.*

experience /ɪkˈspɪriəns/ *n.* an event: *Our visit to Alaska was a pleasant experience.*

make sure /meɪk ʃʊr/ *expression* to make certain: *Make sure to write the grocery list down.*

miss /mɪs/ *v.* to feel a sense of loss: *When the student went to college in a new city, he missed his family.*

_____ _____

_____ _____

Chapter 2

awesome /ˈɒːsəm/ *adj.* creating great admiration: *The size of the Grand Canyon is awesome.*

embarrassed /ɪmˈbærəst/ *adj.* self-conscious or ashamed: *I felt embarrassed when I couldn't understand what the teacher was saying.*

hardly /ˈhɑːrdli/ *adv.* almost not: *We have hardly any money left.*

improve /ɪmˈpruːv/ *v.* to make better: *He improved his appearance by dressing more carefully.*

journal /ˈdʒɜːrnl/ *n.* a written record of the day's events, of one's thoughts and feelings: *She wrote in her journal that she was in love.*

lots /lɑːts/ *n.* a large amount or number: *He has lots of money.*

practice /ˈpræktɪs/ *v.* to do something repeatedly to perfect it: *She practices the piano every day.*

shy /ʃaɪ/ *adj.* not liking to talk to people: *The shy boy stood in a corner at the dance.*

_____ _____

_____ _____

Unit 4
Chapter 1

advice /ədˈvaɪs/ *n.* directions or opinions as given to someone about what to do: *She took my advice and did not drop out of high school.*

average /ˈævərɪdʒ/ *adj.* ordinary, neither very good nor very bad: *He's not excellent; he's just an average child.*

borrow /ˈbɑːroʊ/ *v.* to receive a loan of something with the promise to return it: *She borrowed $2,000 from the bank.*

education /ˌedʒəˈkeɪʃən/ *n.* basic instruction in schools: *The public schools in our neighborhood offer a good education.*

expenses /ɪkˈspensɪz/ *n.* money that must be

paid: *What are your monthly personal expenses?*

list /lɪst/ *v.* to make a list of: *We should list the items we have received.*

personal /ˈpɜːrsənəl/ *adj.* related to a particular person, private: *He receives personal telephone calls at the office.*

worry /ˈwɜːri/ *v.* to feel troubled or fearful: *She worries about the safety of her children at school.*

_____ _____

_____ _____

Chapter 2

earn /ɜːrn/ *v.* to get money or other things by working: *She earns her living as a doctor.*

owe /oʊ/ *v.* to need to pay money to someone: *He owes the landlord last month's rent.*

rent /rent/ *n.* the amount of money paid for the use of a piece of property: *She pays a low rent on that apartment.*

second-hand /ˈsekənd hænd/ *adj.* used by someone else before: *We bought a second-hand car that has 25,000 miles on it.*

split /splɪt/ *v.* to divide among people: *We split a large sandwich.*

stick to /stɪk tuː/ *phrasal verb* to persist, continue: *Is it easy to stick to your budget?*

tax /tæks/ *n.* a necessary payment on income, sales, etc., to the government: *We pay sales and income taxes.*

transportation /ˌtrænspɔːˈteɪʃən/ *n.* ways to move from one place to another: *Transportation by air, rail, and road is easily available in the United States.*

_____ _____

_____ _____

Unit 5
Chapter 1

address /əˈdres/ *v.* to speak about: *She addressed the issue at the meeting.*

attention /əˈtenʃən/ *n.* looking and listening: *His attention to his work was interrupted by the telephone.*

combination /ˌkɑːmbɪˈneɪʃən/ *n.* two or more things, ideas, or events put together: *Chicken soup is a combination of pieces of chicken, vegetables, and water.*

convenient /kənˈviːniənt/ *adj.* easy and comfortable to do or get to: *Our neighborhood is convenient to the stores and subway.*

emergency /ɪˈmɜːrdʒənsi/ *n.* a bad situation that requires immediate attention: *Call the police; this is an emergency!*

impolite /ˌɪmpəˈlaɪt/ *adj.* showing bad manners, rude: *It is impolite to stare at people.*

permission /pərˈmɪʃən/ *n.* agreement to allow someone to do something: *She asked for permission to leave work early.*

sensitive /ˈsensɪtɪv/ *adj.* able to sense or feel in a stronger than normal way: *His skin is sensitive to wool.*

_____ _____

_____ _____

Chapter 2

accident /ˈæksɪdənt/ *n.* something harmful or unpleasant that happens by surprise: *He had an accident on the way to work; he fell and broke an ankle.*

along with /əˈlɔːŋ wɪθ/ *expression* to be together with: *He went along with his girlfriend to the mall.*

broadcast /ˈbrɔːdkæst/ *v.* to send over the air (radio, TV, Internet): *Some radio and TV stations broadcast programs 24 hours a day.*

concern /kənˈsɜːrn/ *n.* care, attention: *He shows constant concern about how his mother is feeling.*

imagine /ɪˈmædʒɪn/ *v.* to form in one's mind: *She imagined what it was like to be rich and famous.*

post /poʊst/ *v.* to put up: *The school principal posted a notice on the bulletin board.*

refuse /rɪˈfjuːz/ *v.* to say no: *He refused an invitation to a party.*

typically /ˈtɪpɪkli/ *adv.* characteristically, representative of: *He was typically late.*

_____ _____

_____ _____

Unit 6
Chapter 1

announce /əˈnaʊns/ *v.* to say something in public: *The parents announced the wedding of their daughter in the newspaper.*

apply /əˈplaɪ/ *v.* to ask for admission or assistance: *I applied to the state university to study.*

government /ˈgʌvərnmənt/ *n.* a system of political control of a country, city, etc.: *That country has a military government.*

guide /gaɪd/ *n.* a reference book: *Please refer to the map guide.*

process /ˈprɒses/ *n.* a procedure, specific method: *The process of filling out an application often takes time.*

require /rɪˈkwaɪr/ *v.* to need: *This radio requires two batteries.*

select /sɪˈlekt/ *v.* to choose specific people or things: *The woman selected a vegetable dish from the menu.*

submit /səbˈmɪt/ *v.* to hand in or give something: *When I finish this short story, I'll submit it to a magazine.*

_____ _____

_____ _____

Chapter 2

hunt /hʌnt/ *v.* to look for something: *I hunted for my hat and finally found it.*

look like /lʊk laɪk/ *expression* to seem probable that: *It looks like (it's going to) snow.*

manage /ˈmænɪdʒ/ *v.* to direct the business of an organization: *She manages a legal department in a large company.*

object /ˈɑːbdʒɪkt/ *n.* the focus: *The object is to place the ball into the net.*

race /reɪs/ *v.* to compete by going faster than someone else: *At a track meet, races are run, such as the 100-meter and 1,500-meter races.*

slide /slaɪd/ *v.* to move something across a surface: *Workers slid boxes across the floor.*

take a wrong turn /teɪk ə rɒːŋ tɜːrn/ *expression* to go in the wrong direction (when driving): *We took a wrong turn and ended up on the other side of the neighborhood.*

take place /teɪk pleɪs/ *expression* to happen, occur: *The town fete takes place once a year.*

_____ _____

_____ _____

Unit 7
Chapter 1

attend /əˈtend/ *v.* to be present at: *I attended the wedding at the church.*

attract /əˈtrækt/ *v.* to create interest: *San Francisco attracts millions of tourists each year.*

contain /kənˈteɪn/ *v.* to hold within something: *That can contains peanuts.*

medicine /ˈmedɪsən/ *n.* the art and science of curing sick people and preventing disease: *Modern medicine can now cure many diseases that used to kill people.*

research /rɪˈsɜːrtʃ/ *n.* a study of information about something: *She did research in a chemical laboratory.*

survive /sərˈvaɪv/ *v.* to continue to live or exist: *This tree has survived for many years.*

train /treɪn/ *v.* to educate, instruct: *Trade schools train students in job skills.*

valuable /ˈvæljʊbəl/ *adj.* having worth, value: *Gold jewelry is valuable.*

_____ _____

_____ _____

Chapter 2

boil /bɔɪl/ *v.* to heat a liquid until it reaches the temperature of 212°F or 100°C: *I boiled the water to cook the eggs.*

century /ˈsentʃəri/ *n.* a time period of 100 years: *Many scientific discoveries were made during the 20th century (1901–2000).*

engineer /ˌendʒɪˈnɪr/ *n.* a person trained in science and mathematics who plans the making of machines, roads, bridges, etc.: *She is an electrical engineer who works for a computer company.*

flood /flʌd/ *v.* to cover dry land with water: *The river ran over its banks and flooded the town.*

prize /praɪz/ *n.* something valuable given to the winner of a competition or game: *First prize in the competition was a new car.*

rotate /ˈroʊteɪt/ *v.* to move around something, especially in a circle: *Planets rotate around the sun.*

threaten /ˈθretn/ *v.* to say you will hurt someone: *A manager threatens to fire an employee unless her work improves.*

wheel /wiːl/ *n.* a round piece of metal, rubber, wood, etc., allowing something to turn and roll: *Cars have four wheels; bicycles have two.*

_____ _____

_____ _____

Unit 8
Chapter 1

admire /ədˈmaɪr/ *v.* to respect, approve of: *I admire how quickly she learned English.*

calculate /ˈkælkjʊleɪt/ *v.* to do math: *Can you calculate how much money we would need for the trip?*

civilization /ˌsɪvələˈzeɪʃən/ *n.* a high level of government, laws, written language, art, music, etc., within a society or culture: *The Mayan civilization lasted about 3,000 years.*

develop /dɪˈveləp/ *v.* to happen, occur: *Before making any plans to travel, let's see what develops when the storm arrives.*

originate /əˈrɪdʒɪneɪt/ *v.* to begin, come from: *Automobiles originated in the 19th century.*

replace /rɪˈpleɪs/ *v.* to take the place of someone or something: *Her boss retired, and she replaced him.*

situation /ˌsɪtʃuˈeɪʃən/ *n.* the way things are at a certain time, what's happening: *The leaders are meeting to talk about the situation in their countries.*

variety /vəˈraɪəti/ *n.* different types of things: *That store carries a wide variety of goods, from clothes to furniture.*

_____ _____

_____ _____

Chapter 2

communicate /kəˈmjuːnɪkeɪt/ *v.* to give information to others: *People communicate with each other by spoken or written language or by body movements.*

formal /ˈfɔːrməl/ *adj.* very or too proper: *He's a difficult person to get to know because he's always so formal.*

get the hang of /get ðə hæŋ əv/ *expression* to understand how to do something: *If you practice hard, you will soon get the hang of it.*

intention /ɪnˈtenʃən/ *n.* purpose, plan: *It was his intention to leave at 6:30, but he stayed until 8:00.*

practical /ˈpræktɪkəl/ *adj.* useful: *A computer would be a practical gift for a student.*

similar /ˈsɪmələr/ *adj.* almost alike: *She has a blue dress similar to yours, but hers has a green collar.*

stand for /stænd fə/ *phrasal verb* to have or represent an idea: *This country stands for life, liberty, and the pursuit of happiness.*

variation /ˌverəriˈeɪʃən/ *n.* a change: *There are different variations of this dish.*

_____ _____

_____ _____

Unit 9
Chapter 1

celebrate /ˈselɪbreɪt/ *v.* to do something special (like having a party) for an occasion: *I celebrated my birthday with friends in my favorite restaurant.*

festival /ˈfestɪvəl/ *n.* a public celebration, usually of some special occasion: *On Norwegian independence day, the Norwegians in my town hold a festival with singing and dancing.*

flashy /ˈflæʃi/ *adj.* showy: *He wears flashy clothes and drives an expensive sports car.*

mask /mæsk/ *n.* a covering for the face used especially to hide one's identity or for a ceremony: *Skiers use masks to keep their faces warm in the cold.*

parade /pəˈreɪd/ *n.* an orderly movement of people in colorful or formal dress or uniforms, usually to show pride or to honor a special day or event: *On Memorial Day, we saw a parade of soldiers marching in honor of those who died in war.*

pleasure /ˈpleʒər/ *n.* enjoyment, the feeling of happiness: *Good food is one of life's great pleasures.*

sacrifice /ˈsækrɪfaɪs/ *n.* loss, or giving up of something valuable, for a purpose: *The parents made many sacrifices, such as wearing old clothes, to pay for their children's education.*

socialize /ˈsouʃəl-aɪz/ *v.* to be with other people in a friendly way for talking, dining, etc.: *We socialize with two other couples almost every weekend.*

_____ _____

_____ _____

Chapter 2

bathe /beɪð/ *v.* to wash oneself: *He bathes daily in the bathtub.*

ceremony /ˈserɪmouni/ *n.* a formal event, usually with rituals: *The priest performed a marriage ceremony.*

discipline /ˈdɪsɪplɪn/ *n.* obedience to rules of good behavior and order: *The students were quiet because their teacher demanded discipline in the classroom.*

flag /flæg/ *n.* a piece of fabric, usually with a design used as a symbol: *The flags of many countries fly near the United Nations building.*

greet /griːt/ *v.* to say hello to someone: *When I met the president, she greeted me in a very friendly way.*

pile /paɪl/ *n.* a collection of similar things laid together, forming the shape of a small hill, a heap: *A truck left a pile of sand near the road.*

pour /pɔːr/ *v.* to let flow in a steady stream: *She poured milk into her coffee.*

sand /sænd/ *n.* tiny pieces of rock, which form the surface of beaches and deserts: *At the beach, we like to dig for shells in the sand.*

_____ _____

_____ _____

Unit 10
Chapter 1

adult /əˈdʌlt/ *n.* a person or animal who has finished growing: *At 21 years of age, he is now an adult.*

allow /əˈlaʊ/ *v.* to let, permit: *We allowed our son to use the family car.*

consider /kənˈsɪdər/ *v.* to think about something: *I will consider your offer and tell you my decision tomorrow.*

gamble /ˈgæmbəl/ *v.* to play games of chance for money: *He gambles on horse races.*

make sense /meɪk sens/ *expression* to be reasonable, logical: *His explanation doesn't make sense.*

prohibit /proʊˈhɪbɪt/ *v.* to forbid, to ban by order or law: *The law prohibits people from killing each other.*

retire /rɪˈtaɪr/ *v.* to leave the workforce and stop working: *At age 70, he retired and moved to Florida.*

transition /trænˈzɪʃən/ *n.* a change from one condition to another: *The transition from high school to college can be difficult for students.*

_____ _____

_____ _____

Chapter 2

freedom /ˈfriːdəm/ *n.* having the power to act or speak without being stopped: *The boy has the freedom to go where he wants to go.*

frequently /ˈfriːkwəntli/ *adv.* often: *Car theft happens frequently in this area.*

frightened /ˈfraɪtnd/ *adj.* feeling afraid: *The child is frightened of dogs.*

gradually /ˈɡrædʒuəli/ *adv.* happening slowly or by small steps: *Gradually, I got used to life in the city.*

independent /ˌɪndɪˈpendənt/ *adj.* free: *The United States became an independent nation in 1776.*

interview /ˈɪntərvjuː/ *v.* to get information by questioning someone: *A TV reporter interviewed the mayor about the city's problems.*

overcome /ˌoʊvərˈkeɪm/ *v.* to fight against something successfully: *He overcame his fear of heights.*

suburb /ˈsʌbɜːrb/ *n.* a small city or town outside a large city: *There are many cars in the suburbs.*

_____ _____

_____ _____

Unit 11
Chapter 1

amuse /əˈmjuːz/ *v.* to please: *Our friend's joke amused us.*

connect /kəˈnekt/ *v.* to put or join together: *I connected the TV antenna to the TV.*

disapprove /ˌdɪsəˈpruːv/ *v.* to have a bad opinion of: *Her father disapproved of her behavior.*

foolishness /ˈfuːlɪʃnɪs/ *adj.* poor judgment: *Her foolishness caused her to lose all her money.*

keep track of /kiːp træk əv/ *expression* to keep an account of, to watch carefully: *Do you keep track of your expenses?*

personality /ˌpɜːrsəˈnælɪti/ *n.* the total effect or character of a person's qualities (habits, behavior, attitudes, etc.): *She has a warm, lively personality.*

reveal /rɪˈviːl/ *v.* to uncover something hidden: *He revealed his secrets to his friend.*

take risks /teɪk rɪsks/ *expression* to take a chance on something: *When you don't fasten your seat belts, you are taking a risk with your life.*

_____ _____

_____ _____

Chapter 2

claim /clæm/ *v.* to state that something is true: *He claimed that he knew who the thief was.*

deserve /dɪˈzɜːrv/ *v.* to be worthy of, earn something good or bad: *A good worker deserves good pay.*

have confidence in /həv ˈkɒnfɪdəns ɪn/ *expression* to be sure of something: *The teacher has a lot of confidence in his students.*

recent /ˈriːsənt/ *adj.* in the past, not very long ago, such as yesterday, last week, last month: *I paid a recent visit to my parents, last month, in fact.*

stress /stres/ *n.* mental or physical pain or difficulty caused by pressure: *She is full of* stress because her boss gives her too much work.

suspicious /səˈspɪʃəs/ *adj.* having suspicions, distrustful of others: *He is suspicious of everyone who disagrees with him.*

take into account /teɪk ˈɪntə əˈkaʊnt/ *expression* to allow or plan for something: *We should take into account that there will be vegetarians at the party, so let's prepare some vegetarian dishes.*

weakness /ˈwiːknɪs/ *n.* lack of strength: *The patient is suffering from weakness after the operation.*

_____ _____

_____ _____

Unit 12
Chapter 1

delight /dɪˈlaɪt/ *n.* happiness, joy: *She jumped up in delight.*

descend /dɪˈsend/ *v.* to go down: *He descended the stairs.*

dish /dɪʃ/ *n.* plates, bowls, and platters used to serve and hold food: *Please put the dishes on the table for dinner.*

greedy /ˈɡriːdi/ *adj.* to desire money, food, etc.: *He is a greedy man. No amount of money will ever be enough for him.*

out of breath /aʊt əv breθ/ *expression* to have difficulty breathing: *After climbing all those stairs, I feel out of breath.*

request /rɪˈkwest/ *v.* to ask for something: *The teacher requested the class to be quiet.*

stairs /sters/ *n.* several steps going up: *I took the stairs to the second floor.*

suddenly /ˈsʌdnli/ *adv.* quickly and unexpectedly: *The girl suddenly started crying, and we did not know what to do.*

_____ _____

_____ _____

Chapter 2

avoid /əˈvɔɪd/ *v.* to stay away from: *She avoids walking on dark streets at night.*

cruel /ˈkruːəl/ *adj.* willing to cause others mental or physical pain, mean: *She makes cruel remarks about her husband being too fat.*

hoax /hoʊks/ *n.* something that is not true, a trick: *The bomb threat turned out to be a hoax.*

immense /ɪˈmens/ *adj.* very large: *There is an immense statue in the park.*

nurse /nɜːrs/ *v.* to give care to sick or old people: *He nursed his wife back to health.*

rescue /ˈreskjuː/ *v.* to save from danger: *Firefighters rescued people from the burning building.*

take in /teɪk ɪn/ *phrasal verb* to give shelter, to care for: *She takes in stray cats who have no home.*

terrible /ˈterəbəl/ *adj.* horrible, very bad: *There was a terrible car accident.*

_____ _____

_____ _____

Maps: North & South America

- Calgary
- Vancouver
- Ottawa
- Toronto
- Lake Placid
- Boston
- Chicago
- New York
- Salt Lake City
- Washington D.C.
- San Francisco
- Louisville
- Los Angeles
- Atlanta
- Phoenix
- New Orleans

Atlantic Ocean

- Havana
- Mexico City
- Kingston
- San Juan
- Panama
- Caracas
- Bogotá

Pacific Ocean

- Lima
- La Paz
- Brasília
- Rio de Janeiro
- São Paulo
- Asunción
- Santlago
- Montevideo
- Buenos Aires

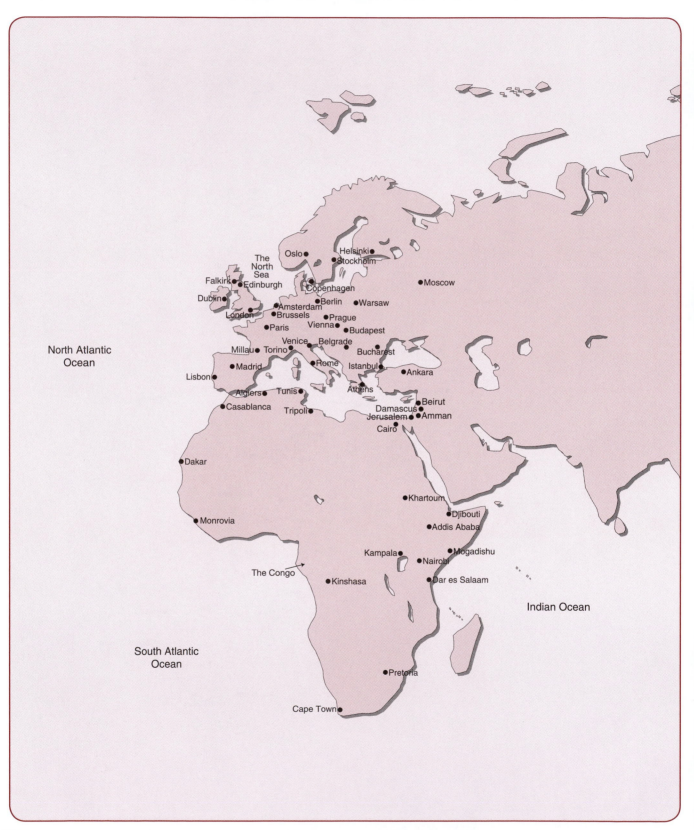

North Atlantic
Ocean

Oslo

Helsinki
Stockholm

The
North
Sea

Falkirk Edinburgh

Moscow

Copenhagen

Dublin

Berlin Warsaw

Amsterdam

London Brussels

Prague

Paris Vienna Budapest

Venice Belgrade

Millau Torino

Bucharest

Rome Istanbul

Lisbon

Madrid

Ankara

Athens

Algiers Tunis

Beirut

Casablanca Tripoli

Damascus Amman

Jerusalem

Cairo

Dakar

Khartoum

Monrovia

Djibouti

Addis Ababa

Kampala Mogadishu

Nairobi

The Congo

Kinshasa Dar es Salaam

Indian Ocean

South Atlantic
Ocean

Pretoria

Cape Town

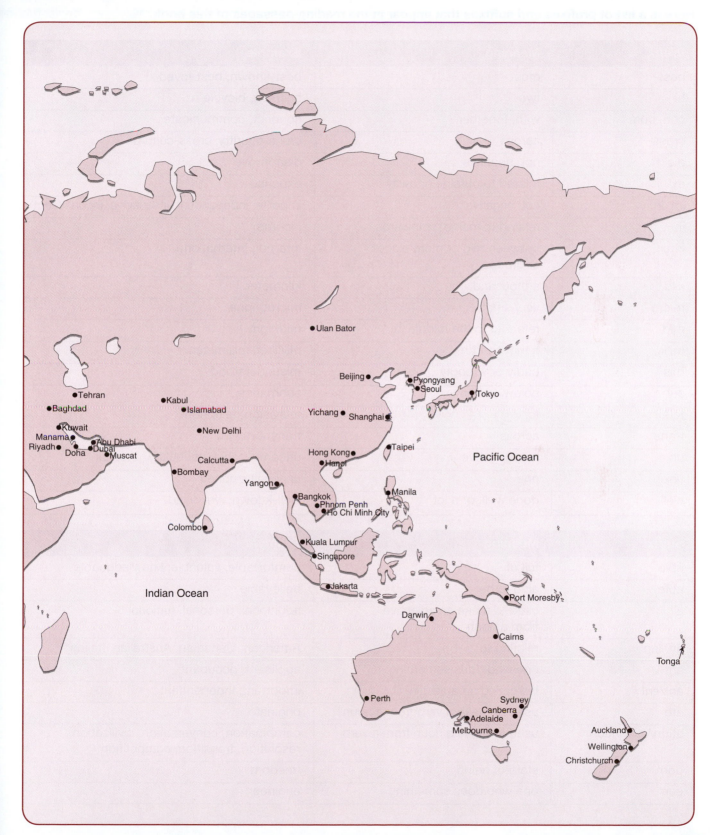

Prefixes and Suffixes

Here is a list of prefixes and suffixes that appear in the reading passages of this book.

Prefix	Meaning	Example
best-	most	best-known, best-loved
bi	two	biathlon, bicycle
con, com	with, together	connect, communicate
cross-	across	cross-country, cross-cultural
dis	not, negative	disapprove
ex	related to outside or away	expense
im, in	not, negative	impolite, independent, insensitive, inconsistent
in	related to inside, or inwards	income
inter	between two or more places or groups	Internet, international
kilo	a thousand	kilometer
micro	very small	microphone
mid	referring to the middle	midnight
milli	a thousandth	milliliter, millimeter
mis	badly or wrongly	misunderstood
sub	below, under	submarine
tele	far	television, telephone
trans	across	transportation
un	not, negative	uncomfortable, unhealthy, unusual
uni	one	university, united
well-	done well, or a lot	well-known, well-liked

Suffix	Meaning	Example
able	full of	comfortable, valuable, knowledgeable
able	able to be	believable
al	used to make an adjective from a noun	additional, personal, national
an, ian	relating to	American, Canadian, Australian, Italian
ant	one who does something	applicant, occupant
ant/ent	indicating an adjective	important, independent
ate	used to make a verb from a noun	originate
ation/ution/ition	used to make a noun from a verb	combination, conversation, civilization, resolution, transition, competition
dom	state of being	freedom
eer	one who does something	engineer

Suffix	Meaning	Example
en	used to form verbs meaning to increase a quality	harden, threaten, frighten
ence	added to some adjectives to make a noun	excellence
ent	used to make an adjective from a verb	excellent
ent	one who does something	student
er, or	someone or something that does something	computer, air conditioner, ringer, reporter, competitor, learner, teacher
er	(after an adjective) more	faster, safer
ese	relating to	Taiwanese, Japanese
est	(after an adjective) most	closest, earliest, thinnest
ever	any	whatever
ful	filled with	harmful, useful, beautiful, colorful, forgetful
hood	state or condition	adulthood, childhood
ion, sion, tion	indicating a noun	opinion, religion, permission, discussion, education, invention
ine	indicating a verb	combine
ish	relating to	British, Irish, foolish
ist	one who does something	terrorist
ity	used to make a noun from an adjective	personality, celebrity
ive	indicating an adjective	expensive, sensitive
ize	used to make a verb from an adjective	socialize
less	without, not having	hopeless
ly	used to form an adverb from an adjective	carefully, frequently
mate	companion	roommate, classmate
ment	used to make a noun from a verb	movement, excitement, requirement, government
ness	used to make a noun from an adjective	foolishness
ous, ious	relating to	adventurous, dangerous, delicious, curious
-shaped	in the shape of	moon-shaped
some	full of	awesome, handsome
th	indicating an order	fifteenth, eighteenth
un	not, negative	unhealthy, unfortunate
ure	indicating some nouns	culture, temperature, candidature
y	indicating an adjective	healthy, flashy

Reading Rate Chart

Time (minutes)	Review Reading 1	2	3	4	5	6	7	8	Rate (words per minute)
1:00									270
1:15									216
1:30									180
1:45									154
2:00									135
2:15									120
2:30									108
2:45									98
3:00									90
3:15									83
3:30									77
3:45									72
4:00									68
4:15									64
4:30									60
4:45									57
5:00									54
5:15									51
5:30									49
5:45									47
6:00									45
6:15									43
6:30									42
6:45									40
7:00									39

Reading Comprehension Chart

Score	Review Reading 1	2	3	4	5	6	7	8
6								
5								
4								
3								
2								
1								
0								